NO FEAR SHAKESPEARE

NO FEAR SHAKESPEARE

As You Like It

The Comedy of Errors

Hamlet

Henry IV, Parts One and Two

Henry V

Julius Caesar

King Lear

Macbeth

The Merchant of Venice

A Midsummer Night's Dream

Much Ado About Nothing

Othello

Richard III

Romeo and Juliet

Sonnets

The Taming of the Shrew

The Tempest

Twelfth Night

NO FEAR SHAKESPEARE

THE COMEDY OF ERRORS

SPARKNOTES is a registered trademark of SparkNotes LLC

Spark Publishing
120 Fifth Avenue
New York, NY 10011

18 **SN** 20

Please submit all comments and questions or report errors to www.sparknotes.com/errors

Printed and bound in the United States

Library of Congress Cataloging-in-Publication Data

Shakespeare, William, 1564–1616.
The comedy of errors/ edited by John Crowther.
p. cm. — (No fear Shakespeare)
Summary: Presents the original text of Shakespeare's play side by side
with a modern version, with marginal notes and explanations and full
descriptions of each character.
ISBN 1-4114-0437-8 (alk.paper)
1. Survival after airplane accidents, shipwrecks, etc.—Drama. 2. Mistaken
identity—Drama. 3. Brothers—Drama. 4. Greece—Drama. 5. Twins—Drama.
I. Crowther, John (John C.) II. Title. III. Series.
PR2804.A2C76 2005
822.3'3—dc22   2005006772

There's matter in these sighs, these profound heaves.
You must translate: 'tis fit we understand them.

(*Hamlet*, 4.1.1–2)

FEAR NOT.

Have you ever found yourself looking at a Shakespeare play, then down at the footnotes, then back at the play, and still not understanding? You know what the individual words mean, but they don't add up. SparkNotes' *No Fear Shakespeare* will help you break through all that. Put the pieces together with our easy-to-read translations. Soon you'll be reading Shakespeare's own words fearlessly—and actually enjoying it.

No Fear Shakespeare puts Shakespeare's language side-by-side with a facing-page translation into modern English— the kind of English people actually speak today. When Shakespeare's words make your head spin, our translation will help you sort out what's happening, who's saying what, and why.

THE COMEDY OF ERRORS

CHARACTERS

Antipholus of Syracuse—The twin brother of Antipholus of Ephesus and the son of Egeon. Antipholus of Syracuse has been traveling the world with his slave, Dromio of Syracuse, trying to find his long-lost brother and mother. At the beginning of the play, he has just arrived in Ephesus. The years of searching have made this Antipholus restless and anxious: he worries that in searching for his lost family members, he has somehow lost himself. When confronted with the Ephesians' strange behavior, Antipholus's disorientation is intensified—he cannot tell whether he should be terrified of their seemingly supernatural powers or thankful for the gifts they bestow upon him.

Antipholus of Ephesus—The twin brother of Antipholus of Syracuse. Antipholus of Ephesus is married to Adriana and is a well-respected merchant in Ephesus. He owns a house called the Phoenix and is the head of a large and bustling household. Having served bravely in his army, Antipholus of Ephesus is a favorite of Duke Solinus. Unlike his twin brother, Antipholus of Ephesus is very settled and well established: he has much to lose in the confusion and chaos.

Dromio of Syracuse and **Dromio of Ephesus**—Long-lost twin brothers and servants to Antipholus of Syracuse and Antipholus of Ephesus, respectively. The Dromio twins are more nearly identical to each other than the Antipholus twins. Witty, antic, and perennially put upon, they grumblingly but good-naturedly endure endless abuse from their masters and mistresses. The Dromio twins' history resembles that of the Antipholus twins: they were born on the same day as their masters, a fact that is referenced often in the text. However, the resemblance between servant and master ends there. Despite the play's frantic substitutions and frequent cases of mistaken identity, the line between master and servant is one that is never crossed.

Adriana—The wife of Antipholus of Ephesus and a fiercely jealous woman. Adriana doesn't appreciate or put much stock in her sister, Luciana's, advice to be meek and accommodating toward her husband, whom Adriana believes is cheating on her.

Luciana—Adriana's unmarried sister and the object of Antipholus of Syracuse's affections. Luciana preaches the virtues of patience and subservience to her sisters.

Egeon—An elderly Syracusian merchant. Egeon is the long-lost husband of the abbess Emilia and the father of the two Antipholus twins. As the play begins, Egeon has been sentenced to death for violating a law prohibiting travel between Syracuse and Ephesus. He had been searching for the son he raised, who left Syracuse seven years ago to find their missing family members.

Abbess—The head of a religious order in Ephesus. The abbess's real name is Emilia, and she is the long-lost wife of Egeon and the mother of the Antipholus twins.

Duke Solinus—The ruler of Ephesus.

Balthasar—A merchant in Ephesus.

Angelo—A goldsmith in Ephesus and a friend to Antipholus of Ephesus.

Merchant—An Ephesian friend of Antipholus of Syracuse. The merchant cautions Antipholus of Syracuse to disguise himself so as to escape the punishment reserved for Syracusian travelers.

Second Merchant—A tradesman to whom Angelo is in debt.

Doctor Pinch—A schoolteacher, doctor, and would-be exorcist.

Nell—Antipholus of Ephesus's obese kitchen maid and Dromio of Ephesus's wife. Nell never appears onstage, but Dromio of Syracuse gives a lengthy description of her.

Luce—A maid to Antipholus of Ephesus. Along with Dromio of Syracuse, Luce keeps her master out of the Phoenix while his wife and his twin brother are dining inside. Some editions call this character "Nell," thereby combining her with Dromio of Ephesus's fat wife.

Courtesan—A friend of Antipholus of Ephesus and proprietress of the Porpentine.

ACT ONE
SCENE 1

Enter the DUKE, EGEON, JAILER, *and other attendants*

EGEON

    Proceed, Solinus, to procure my fall,
    And by the doom of death end woes and all.

DUKE SOLINUS

    Merchant of Syracuse, plead no more.
    I am not partial to infringe our laws.
5   The enmity and discord which of late
    Sprung from the rancorous outrage of your duke
    To merchants, our well-dealing countrymen,
    Who, wanting guilders to redeem their lives,
    Have seal'd his rigorous statutes with their bloods,
10   Excludes all pity from our threatening looks.
    For, since the mortal and intestine jars
    'Twixt thy seditious countrymen and us,
    It hath in solemn synods been decreed
    Both by the Syracusians and ourselves,
15   To admit no traffic to our adverse towns.
    Nay, more, if any born at Ephesus
    Be seen at any Syracusian marts and fairs;
    Again, if any Syracusian born
    Come to the bay of Ephesus, he dies,
20   His goods confiscate to the Duke's dispose,
    Unless a thousand marks be levièd
    To quit the penalty and to ransom him.
    Thy substance, valued at the highest rate,
    Cannot amount unto a hundred marks;
25   Therefore by law thou art condemned to die.

EGEON

    Yet this my comfort: when your words are done,
    My woes end likewise with the evening sun.

ACT ONE
SCENE 1

The DUKE, EGEON, *and the* JAILER *enter, with other attendants.*

EGEON

Continue, Solinus, and bring on my downfall. Give me the death sentence and end all my troubles.

DUKE

Merchant of Syracuse, stop your begging: I'm not inclined to bend our laws. The hatred and discord between our two cities is the result of the bitter offenses your duke has perpetrated against the merchants of Ephesus, our well-behaved countrymen. Lacking the money to ransom themselves, these merchants were executed under your duke's harsh laws, and this has erased all looks of pity from my face. Ever since these deadly conflicts erupted between your violent countrymen and ours, both you Syracusians and we Ephesians have held serious councils and decided not to permit any travel between our two hostile towns. No—the law goes further: if anyone born in Ephesus is seen in Syracuse's marketplaces or if anyone born in Syracuse comes to Ephesus, that man dies, and his possessions will be confiscated by the Duke, unless he can raise a thousand marks to pay the penalty and ransom himself. Your possessions, even if we calculate their worth very generously, don't even add up to a hundred marks. Therefore, by law, you are condemned to die.

EGEON

At least I have this comfort: when you finish speaking, my troubles will also end, at sundown.

DUKE SOLINUS

Well, Syracusian, say in brief the cause
Why thou departedst from thy native home
30   And for what cause thou camest to Ephesus.

EGEON

A heavier task could not have been imposed
Than I to speak my griefs unspeakable;
Yet, that the world may witness that my end
Was wrought by nature, not by vile offense,
35   I'll utter what my sorrow gives me leave.
In Syracusa was I born, and wed
Unto a woman happy but for me,
And by me, had not our hap been bad.
With her I lived in joy. Our wealth increased
40   By prosperous voyages I often made
To Epidamnum, till my factor's death
And the great care of goods at random left
Drew me from kind embracements of my spouse;
From whom my absence was not six months old
45   Before herself—almost at fainting under
The pleasing punishment that women bear—
Had made provision for her following me
And soon and safe arrivèd where I was.
There had she not been long but she became
50   A joyful mother of two goodly sons,
And, which was strange, the one so like the other
As could not be distinguished but by names.
That very hour, and in the selfsame inn,
A meaner woman was deliverèd
55   Of such a burden, male twins, both alike.
Those, for their parents were exceeding poor,
I bought and brought up to attend my sons.
My wife, not meanly proud of two such boys,
Made daily motions for our home return.
60   Unwilling, I agreed. Alas, too soon
We came aboard.

DUKE

Well, Syracusian, tell us—briefly—why you left your hometown and came to Ephesus.

EGEON

Asking me to speak of my unspeakable griefs—that's the hardest task you could impose on me. But I'll do it so that the world can see that it was natural emotion, and not a desire to break the law, that brought me to this fate. I'll tell you whatever my sorrow permits me to say. I was born in Syracuse, and I married a woman—a fortunate woman, except for having been married to me. And yet I would have made her happy had our luck not been so bad. I lived with her in joy, and our wealth increased from the prosperous journeys I frequently made to Epidamnum. Then my agent died and, obligated to care for my now untended goods abroad, I was drawn away from my wife's fond embraces. I hadn't been gone for six months when my wife, almost fainting with the pains of pregnancy, made arrangements to follow me, and she soon arrived safely where I was. She hadn't been there very long before she became the joyful mother of twin boys. It was strange: they looked so much alike that the only way to tell them apart was by their names. In the same hour, and in the same inn, a poor woman also delivered identical twin boys. Their parents had very little, so I bought the boys and raised them as companions and servants for our twin sons. My wife was more than a little proud of our two boys, and every day she would press me to return home. Reluctantly, I agreed—alas! Too quickly, we boarded a ship.

A league from Epidamnum had we sailed
Before the always-wind-obeying deep
Gave any tragic instance of our harm;
But longer did we not retain much hope;
For what obscured light the heavens did grant
Did but convey unto our fearful minds
A doubtful warrant of immediate death,
Which though myself would gladly have embraced,
Yet the incessant weepings of my wife,
Weeping before for what she saw must come,
And piteous plainings of the pretty babes,
That mourned for fashion, ignorant what to fear,
Forced me to seek delays for them and me.
And this it was, for other means was none:
The sailors sought for safety by our boat
And left the ship, then sinking-ripe, to us.
My wife, more careful for the latter-born,
Had fastened him unto a small spare mast,
Such as seafaring men provide for storms.
To him one of the other twins was bound,
Whilst I had been like heedful of the other.
The children thus disposed, my wife and I,
Fixing our eyes on whom our care was fixed,
Fastened ourselves at either end the mast
And, floating straight, obedient to the stream,
Was carried towards Corinth, as we thought.
At length the sun, gazing upon the earth,
Dispersed those vapors that offended us,
And by the benefit of his wished light
The seas waxed calm, and we discoverèd
Two ships from far, making amain to us,
Of Corinth that, of Epidaurus this.
But ere they came,—O, let me say no more!
Gather the sequel by that went before.

league = about three miles

We had sailed a league away from Epidamnum before the sea, which always obeys the winds' commands, gave any indication of danger. We didn't stay hopeful much longer: soon, the sky grew so dark that we were convinced we were going to die immediately. I could have accepted that, but I was forced by my wife's incessant weeping—she wept in advance for the things that she saw ahead—and the piteous complaints of the sweet infants—who cried in imitation of the adults, without understanding why—to find a way to save us. Here's the best I could do: the crew of our ship had fled for safety in the lifeboats and left us to sink with the ship. My wife, who was very concerned about the younger of our twins, tied him to a spare mast—the kind that sailors use for just such a purpose. She tied one of the other twins to him. I did the same with the remaining two boys. With the children taken care of, my wife and I tied ourselves to opposite ends of the mast and floated off, obedient to the current. It carried us toward Corinth—or so we thought. Eventually the sun, looking down upon the earth, burned off the threatening storm clouds. By the power of the sun's wished-for light, the seas became calm. We saw two ships sailing toward us, one from Corinth, the other from Epidaurus. But before they reached us—let me say no more! You'll have to imagine what came next, based on what had already happened.

DUKE SOLINUS

> Nay, forward, old man. Do not break off so,
> For we may pity though not pardon thee.

EGEON

> O, had the gods done so, I had not now
> Worthily termed them merciless to us.
> For, ere the ships could meet by twice five leagues,
> We were encounterd by a mighty rock,
> Which being violently borne upon,
> Our helpful ship was splitted in the midst;
> So that, in this unjust divorce of us,
> Fortune had left to both of us alike
> What to delight in, what to sorrow for.
> Her part, poor soul, seeming as burdenèd
> With lesser weight, but not with lesser woe,
> Was carried with more speed before the wind,
> And in our sight they three were taken up
> By fishermen of Corinth, as we thought.
> At length, another ship had seized on us
> And, knowing whom it was their hap to save,
> Gave healthful welcome to their shipwracked guests,
> And would have reft the fishers of their prey
> Had not their bark been very slow of sail;
> And therefore homeward did they bend their course.
> Thus have you heard me severed from my bliss;
> That by misfortunes was my life prolonged
> To tell sad stories of my own mishaps.

DUKE SOLINUS

> And for the sake of them thou sorrowest for,
> Do me the favour to dilate at full
> What hath befall'n of them and thee till now.

EGEON

> My youngest boy, and yet my eldest care,
> At eighteen years became inquisitive
> After his brother, and importuned me
> That his attendant—so his case was like,

DUKE

No, keep going, old man; don't stop like that. For we may take pity on you, even if we can't pardon you.

EGEON

Had the gods taken pity on us, I wouldn't be here calling them merciless. The two ships hadn't come within ten leagues of us when our ship hit a huge rock and split down the middle. As we were unjustly separated from each other, both my wife and I were left with something to delight in and something to sorrow over. For her part—the poor soul! Her half of the mast weighed less, but she was no luckier than I was: the wind carried her away more quickly. I saw them rescued by fishermen from Corinth—or so I thought. After a while, another ship rescued me and the two boys who were with me. The sailors knew me, so they took good care of us. Our ship would have caught up with the other ship and taken back my wife and the children, but we sailed too slowly and their ship sped toward their home. So now you've heard how I was separated from everything I love. It's been my bad luck to remain alive long enough to be able to tell the sad stories of my own misfortunes.

DUKE

And for the sake of those you grieve for, do me a favor: tell me the full story of what has happened to you and them, up to this point.

EGEON

My youngest son, whom I care about the most, turned eighteen and started to wonder about his twin brother. He asked me to let him take his attendant—who had also lost a brother, though he had kept his

Reft of his brother, but retained his name—
Might bear him company in the quest of him,
130 Whom whilst I laboured of a love to see,
I hazarded the loss of whom I loved.
Five summers have I spent in farthest Greece,
Roaming clean through the bounds of Asia,
And, coasting homeward, came to Ephesus,
135 Hopeless to find, yet loath to leave unsought
Or that or any place that harbors men.
But here must end the story of my life;
And happy were I in my timely death
Could all my travels warrant me they live.

DUKE SOLINUS
140 Hapless Egeon, whom the fates have marked
To bear the extremity of dire mishap,
Now, trust me, were it not against our laws,
Against my crown, my oath, my dignity,
Which princes, would they, may not disannul,
145 My soul would sue as advocate for thee.
But though thou art adjudgèd to the death,
And passèd sentence may not be recalled
But to our honour's great disparagement,
Yet will I favor thee in what I can.
150 Therefore, merchant, I'll limit thee this day
To seek thy life by beneficial help.
Try all the friends thou hast in Ephesus;
Beg thou, or borrow, to make up the sum,
And live. If no, then thou art doom'd to die.—
155 Jailer, take him to thy custody.

JAILER
I will, my lord.

EGEON
Hopeless and helpless doth Egeon wend,
But to procrastinate his lifeless end.

Exeunt

brother's name for himself—and go in search of him.
I wanted to see my lost son as well, so I risked losing
the one I loved in order to find the other. I've spent five
years in the remotest parts of Greece and roaming all
over Asia. On my way home, I came to Ephesus. I
have no hope of finding my boys here, but I will check
every place that is inhabited by men. But that is where
the story of my life must end. I'd be happy to die if, in
all my travels, I could prove that they are alive.

DUKE

Poor Egeon! Fate has decreed that you must endure
the extremes of terrible misfortune. Believe me, if it
weren't against the law, my crown, my duty, and my
position (which princes cannot disobey, not matter
how they feel), my very soul would argue your case.
But you are sentenced to death, and changing a sentence that's already been passed would dishonor my
title. However, I'll do what I can for you. I will allow
you one day to look for help in Ephesus. Call any
friends you have. Beg or borrow to come up with the
ransom. If you can, you live. If not, you are doomed to
die. Jailer, take him into custody.

JAILER

I will.

EGEON

Hopeless and helpless, I go my way, merely putting
off my fatal end.

They exit.

ACT 1, SCENE 2

Enter ANTIPHOLUS OF SYRACUSE, DROMIO OF SYRACUSE, *and*
FIRST MERCHANT

FIRST MERCHANT
Therefore give out you are of Epidamnum,
Lest that your goods too soon be confiscate.
This very day a Syracusian merchant
Is apprehended for arrival here
5   And, not being able to buy out his life,
According to the statute of the town
Dies ere the weary sun set in the west.
There is your money that I had to keep.

ANTIPHOLUS OF SYRACUSE
Go bear it to the Centaur, where we host,
10   And stay there, Dromio, till I come to thee.
Within this hour it will be dinnertime.
Till that, I'll view the manners of the town,
Peruse the traders, gaze upon the buildings,
And then return and sleep within mine inn,
15   For with long travel I am stiff and weary.
Get thee away.

DROMIO OF SYRACUSE
Many a man would take you at your word
And go indeed, having so good a mean.
                                    Exit DROMIO OF SYRACUSE

ANTIPHOLUS OF SYRACUSE
A trusty villain, sir, that very oft,
20   When I am dull with care and melancholy,
Lightens my humor with his merry jests.
What, will you walk with me about the town
And then go to my inn and dine with me?

FIRST MERCHANT
I am invited, sir, to certain merchants,
25   Of whom I hope to make much benefit.

ACT 1, SCENE 2

ANTIPHOLUS OF SYRACUSE, DROMIO OF SYRACUSE, *and* FIRST MERCHANT *enter.*

FIRST MERCHANT

So, tell people that you're from Epidamnum—otherwise all your goods will be confiscated. Just today, a merchant from Syracuse was arrested for coming here. He couldn't afford the ransom, so by law, he'll be put to death before the sun sets. Here's the money you asked me to hold.

ANTIPHOLUS OF SYRACUSE

Dromio, bring this money to the Centaur Inn, where we're lodging, and wait there until I come. It'll be lunchtime within an hour. Until then, I'll walk around town, peruse the markets, and gaze upon the buildings, and then I'll return and sleep at the inn. I'm stiff and weary from all this travel. Get going now.

DROMIO OF SYRACUSE

Many men would take you literally and take off with all this money.

DROMIO OF SYRACUSE *exits.*

ANTIPHOLUS OF SYRACUSE

He's a trustworthy servant. Often, when I'm dulled by worry and melancholy, he lightens my mood with his merry pranks. Listen, will you walk with me around the town and then dine with me at the inn?

FIRST MERCHANT

Begging your pardon, but I've been invited to see some merchants, who I'm hoping to see a profit from.

I crave your pardon. Soon at five o'clock,
Please you, I'll meet with you upon the mart
And afterward consort you till bedtime.
My present business calls me from you now.

ANTIPHOLUS OF SYRACUSE
30   Farewell till then. I will go lose myself
And wander up and down to view the city.

FIRST MERCHANT
Sir, I commend you to your own content.

Exit FIRST MERCHANT

ANTIPHOLUS OF SYRACUSE
He that commends me to mine own content
Commends me to the thing I cannot get.
35   I to the world am like a drop of water
That in the ocean seeks another drop,
Who, falling there to find his fellow forth,
Unseen, inquisitive, confounds himself.
So I, to find a mother and a brother,
40   In quest of them, unhappy, lose myself.

Enter DROMIO OF EPHESUS

Here comes the almanac of my true date.—
What now? How chance thou art returned so soon?

DROMIO OF EPHESUS
Returned so soon? Rather approach'd too late!
The capon burns; the pig falls from the spit;
45   The clock hath strucken twelve upon the bell;
My mistress made it one upon my cheek.
She is so hot because the meat is cold;
The meat is cold because you come not home;
You come not home because you have no stomach;
50   You have no stomach, having broke your fast;
But we that know what 'tis to fast and pray
Are penitent for your default today.

But if it pleases you, I'll meet you in the marketplace at five and will keep you company until bedtime. Right now, my pressing business calls me away.

ANTIPHOLUS OF SYRACUSE
Farewell till then. I will go lose myself, wandering up and down throughout the city.

FIRST MERCHANT
Sir, I leave you to your own contentment.

FIRST MERCHANT *exits.*

ANTIPHOLUS OF SYRACUSE
He leaves me to my own contentment, but that's the one thing I cannot find. Out in the world, I'm like a drop of water, trying to find a drop that matches in the whole wide ocean. When that drop fails its task— unnoticed, inquisitive—it dissipates into the ocean and destroys itself. In order to find a mother and a brother, I too have lost myself, unhappily.

DROMIO OF EPHESUS *enters.*

Here comes the man who shares my birthday. What is it? How is it that you've come back so soon?

DROMIO OF EPHESUS
Back so soon? Too late is more like it. The chicken is burning, the pig is overcooked, the clock has already struck twelve, and my mistress has clocked me one on the cheek. She's hot because lunch is cold; lunch is cold because you're not home; you're not home because you're not hungry; you're not hungry because you've eaten already. But we servants—who know how to properly fast and pray—are being punished for your offenses today.

ANTIPHOLUS OF SYRACUSE
Stop in your wind, sir. Tell me this, I pray:
Where have you left the money that I gave you?

DROMIO OF EPHESUS
55 O, sixpence, that I had o' Wednesday last
To pay the saddler for my mistress' crupper?
The saddler had it, sir; I kept it not.

ANTIPHOLUS OF SYRACUSE
I am not in a sportive humor now.
Tell me, and dally not: where is the money?
60 We being strangers here, how dar'st thou trust
So great a charge from thine own custody?

DROMIO OF EPHESUS
I pray you, jest, sir, as you sit at dinner.
I from my mistress come to you in post;
If I return, I shall be post indeed,
65 For she will scour your fault upon my pate.
Methinks your maw, like mine, should be your clock,
And strike you home without a messenger.

ANTIPHOLUS OF SYRACUSE
Come, Dromio, come, these jests are out of season.
Reserve them till a merrier hour than this.
70 Where is the gold I gave in charge to thee?

DROMIO OF EPHESUS
To me, sir? Why, you gave no gold to me!

ANTIPHOLUS OF SYRACUSE
Come on, sir knave, have done your foolishness,
And tell me how thou hast disposed thy charge.

DROMIO OF EPHESUS
My charge was but to fetch you from the mart
75 Home to your house, the Phoenix, sir, to dinner.
My mistress and her sister stays for you.

ANTIPHOLUS OF SYRACUSE
Now, as I am a Christian, answer me
In what safe place you have bestowed my money,

ANTIPHOLUS OF SYRACUSE

Hold on a second. Answer me this, please: where's the money I gave you?

DROMIO OF EPHESUS

Oh, the sixpence you gave me last Wednesday to buy leather goods for my mistress? The saddle maker has it, sir—I didn't keep it.

ANTIPHOLUS OF SYRACUSE

I'm not in a joking mood. Tell me right now and stop fooling: where's the money? We're strangers here. How dare you let such a large amount escape your keeping?

DROMIO OF EPHESUS

Please, sir; crack jokes over lunch. My mistress made me hurry here. If I go back without you, she'll punish your faults by breaking my head open. I should think that your appetite would act like a clock (as mine does) and bring you home on its own, without the need for a messenger.

ANTIPHOLUS OF SYRACUSE

That's enough, Dromio, please. This isn't a good moment for jokes—save them till a happier time. Where's the gold I gave you?

DROMIO OF EPHESUS

Gave me, sir? You didn't give me any gold.

ANTIPHOLUS OF SYRACUSE

Come on, you rogue. Quit joking. Tell me what you've done with the money I entrusted to you.

DROMIO OF EPHESUS

The only thing that I've been entrusted with was getting you from the market and bringing you to your house, the Phoenix, for lunch. My mistress and her sister are waiting for you.

ANTIPHOLUS OF SYRACUSE

Tell me where you've stowed away my money, or I swear I'll break that comical head of yours for goofing

Or I shall break that merry sconce of yours
80   That stands on tricks when I am undisposed.
Where is the thousand marks thou hadst of me?

DROMIO OF EPHESUS
I have some marks of yours upon my pate,
Some of my mistress' marks upon my shoulders,
But not a thousand marks between you both.
85   If I should pay your worship those again,
Perchance you will not bear them patiently.

ANTIPHOLUS OF SYRACUSE
Thy mistress' marks? what mistress, slave, hast thou?

DROMIO OF EPHESUS
Your worship's wife, my mistress at the Phoenix,
She that doth fast till you come home to dinner
90   And prays that you will hie you home to dinner.

ANTIPHOLUS OF SYRACUSE
What, wilt thou flout me thus unto my face,
Being forbid? There, take you that, sir knave. *(beats* DROMIO
OF EPHESUS*)*

DROMIO OF EPHESUS
What mean you, sir? For God's sake, hold your hands.
Nay, an you will not, sir, I'll take my heels.

                                        Exit DROMIO OF EPHESUS

ANTIPHOLUS OF SYRACUSE
95   Upon my life, by some device or other
The villain is o'erraught of all my money.
They say this town is full of cozenage,
As nimble jugglers that deceive the eye,
Dark-working sorcerers that change the mind,
100   Soul-killing witches that deform the body,
Disguised cheaters, prating mountebanks,
And many suchlike liberties of sin.
If it prove so, I will be gone the sooner.
I'll to the Centaur to go seek this slave.
105   I greatly fear my money is not safe.

                                                        Exit

marks = units
of currency
——————→

when I'm not in the mood. Where are the thousand marks you had from me?

DROMIO OF EPHESUS

I have some marks from you on my head and some of my mistress's marks on my body. But between the both of you, I don't have a thousand marks. If I gave those marks back to you, chances are you wouldn't take them as patiently as I did.

ANTIPHOLUS OF SYRACUSE

Your mistress's marks? What mistress do you have?

DROMIO OF EPHESUS

Your wife, sir. My mistress. At the Phoenix. The one who's waiting for you to come home for lunch and praying that you'll get home quickly.

ANTIPHOLUS OF SYRACUSE

What, are you going to mock me to my face when I told you not to? There, take that, you scoundrel! (*beats* **DROMIO OF EPHESUS**)

DROMIO OF EPHESUS

What are you doing? Stop, for God's sake! Well, if you don't, then I'm out of here.

DROMIO OF EPHESUS *exits.*

ANTIPHOLUS OF SYRACUSE

I swear, somehow the fool has been cheated out of all my money. They say that this town is full of deception—illusionists that can fool the eye, dark sorcerers who can bewitch your mind, soul-killing witches who can disfigure your body, disguised swindlers, fast-talking fakers, and all kinds of other unchecked sins. If this is true, then I'll be leaving all the sooner.

I'll go to the Centaur to find this servant of mine—I fear that my money isn't safe.

He exits.

ACT TWO
SCENE 1

Enter ADRIANA *and* LUCIANA

ADRIANA
> Neither my husband nor the slave returned
> That in such haste I sent to seek his master?
> Sure, Luciana, it is two o'clock.

LUCIANA
> Perhaps some merchant hath invited him,
5 > And from the mart he's somewhere gone to dinner.
> Good sister, let us dine and never fret.
> A man is master of his liberty;
> Time is their master, and when they see time
> They'll go or come. If so, be patient, sister.

ADRIANA
10 > Why should their liberty than ours be more?

LUCIANA
> Because their business still lies out o' door.

ADRIANA
> Look when I serve him so, he takes it ill.

LUCIANA
> O, know he is the bridle of your will.

ADRIANA
> There's none but asses will be bridled so.

LUCIANA
15 > Why, headstrong liberty is lashed with woe.
> There's nothing situate under heaven's eye
> But hath his bound, in earth, in sea, in sky.
> The beasts, the fishes, and the wingèd fowls
> Are their males' subjects and at their controls.
20 > Man, more divine, the masters of all these,

ACT TWO

SCENE 1

ADRIANA *and* LUCIANA *enter.*

ADRIANA

Neither my husband nor the slave has returned, even though I sent the slave off running. Surely, Luciana, it's already two o'clock.

LUCIANA

Maybe some merchant at the marketplace invited him home for lunch. Sister, let's eat and stop worrying. A man is master of his own freedom: time is his only master, and when the right moment comes along, he'll come or go as he pleases. If this is so, be patient, sister.

ADRIANA

Why should men be more free than women?

LUCIANA

Because their business lies outside the home.

ADRIANA

Listen, when I behave this way toward him, he hates it.

LUCIANA

Oh, you should know that he's the bridle to your will.

bridle = muzzle-
like device used to
restrain a horse

ADRIANA

Only a mule would agree to that.

LUCIANA

Why, too much freedom leads to woe. There's nothing under heaven that doesn't have its limits. The beasts on the earth, the fish in the sea, and the birds in the sky are all subject to the males of their species and under their control. Men, who are nearest to God, are the masters of all these creatures. And men—the lords of

Lord of the wide world and wild wat'ry seas,
Endued with intellectual sense and souls,
Of more preeminence than fish and fowls,
Are masters to their females, and their lords.
25   Then let your will attend on their accords.

ADRIANA
This servitude makes you to keep unwed.

LUCIANA
Not this, but troubles of the marriage bed.

ADRIANA
But, were you wedded, you would bear some sway.

LUCIANA
Ere I learn love, I'll practice to obey.

ADRIANA
30   How if your husband start some otherwhere?

LUCIANA
Till he come home again, I would forbear.

ADRIANA
Patience unmoved! No marvel though she pause;
They can be meek that have no other cause.
A wretched soul, bruised with adversity
35   We bid be quiet when we hear it cry,
But were we burdened with like weight of pain,
As much or more we should ourselves complain.
So thou, that hast no unkind mate to grieve thee,
With urging helpless patience would relieve me;
40   But, if thou live to see like right bereft,
This fool-begged patience in thee will be left.

LUCIANA
Well, I will marry one day, but to try.
Here comes your man. Now is your husband nigh.

the wide world and the wild watery seas,
gifted with intellectual sense and souls, greater than
the fish and the birds—are the masters of women and
their lords. Therefore, you should obey their wishes.

ADRIANA

It's this servantlike mentality that's keeping you
unmarried.

LUCIANA

No, that's not it—it's because of what happens in the
marriage bed.

ADRIANA

But if you were married, you'd wield some influence.

LUCIANA

Before I learn how to love, I'll learn how to follow
orders.

ADRIANA

What if your husband strays elsewhere?

LUCIANA

I'd endure it until he came home again.

ADRIANA

Now that's patience! No wonder she's waiting to get
married. It's easy to preach meekness when you have
no reason to act otherwise. When we're faced with a
wretched person, bruised and crying with hardship,
we try to get them to shush up. And yet, if we were suffering the same kind of pain, we'd complain just as
much—if not more! So you, who have no husband
causing you problems, want to comfort me by preach-
ing the virtue of feeble patience. But if you live to see
yourself similarly denied your rights, this foolish
patience will abandon you.

LUCIANA

Well, I'll get married one day, just to see. Here comes
your servant—your husband must be coming soon.

Enter DROMIO OF EPHESUS

ADRIANA
Say, is your tardy master now at hand?

DROMIO OF EPHESUS
45   Nay, he's at two hands with me, and that my two ears can
witness.

ADRIANA
Say, didst thou speak with him? Know'st thou his mind?

DROMIO OF EPHESUS
Ay, ay, he told his mind upon mine ear.
Beshrew his hand, I scarce could understand it.

LUCIANA
50   Spake he so doubtfully thou couldst not feel his meaning?

DROMIO OF EPHESUS
Nay, he struck so plainly I could too well feel his blows, and
withal so doubtfully that I could scarce understand them.

ADRIANA
But say, I prithee, is he coming home?
It seems he hath great care to please his wife.

DROMIO OF EPHESUS
55   Why, mistress, sure my master is horn mad.

ADRIANA
Horn mad, thou villain!

DROMIO OF EPHESUS
                                    I mean not cuckold mad,
But sure he is stark mad.
When I desired him to come home to dinner,
He asked me for a thousand marks in gold.
60   "'Tis dinnertime," quoth I. "My gold," quoth he.

DROMIO OF EPHESUS *enters.*

ADRIANA

Tell me, is your tardy master close at hand?

DROMIO OF EPHESUS

i.e., "He beat me on my ears."

No; but he came at me with two hands—just ask my ears.

ADRIANA

Did you talk to him? Do you know his plans?

DROMIO OF EPHESUS

Dromio puns on "understand," using the word to mean "stand up under the force of the beating."

Yes, yes, he told me his plans on my ears. Damn his hands—I could barely understand it.

LUCIANA

Did he speak so ambiguously that you couldn't get a feeling for what he meant?

DROMIO OF EPHESUS

No; he hit me very clearly and I felt his punches perfectly well. They were so dreadful, I could barely stand up under them.

ADRIANA

But please, tell me: is he coming home? It seems he has taken great care to please his wife.

DROMIO OF EPHESUS

Why, mistress, my master is as angry as a bull with horns.

ADRIANA

Horns? You bastard!

DROMIO OF EPHESUS

cuckold = a man whose wife cheated on him; cuckolds were commonly depicted wearing horns

I don't mean he's cuckold mad. But he sure is angry. When I asked him to come home to lunch, he asked me for a thousand marks. "It's lunchtime," I said. "My gold," he said. "The meat's burning," I said. "My gold," he said. "Will you come home?" I said.

"Your meat doth burn," quoth I. "My gold," quoth he.
"Will you come?" quoth I. "My gold," quoth he.
"Where is the thousand marks I gave thee, villain?"
"The pig," quoth I, "is burned." "My gold," quoth he.
65 "My mistress, sir," quoth I. "Hang up thy mistress!
I know not thy mistress. Out on thy mistress!"

LUCIANA
Quoth who?

DROMIO OF EPHESUS
Quoth my master.
"I know," quoth he, "no house, no wife, no mistress."
70 So that my errand, due unto my tongue,
I thank him, I bare home upon my shoulders,
For, in conclusion, he did beat me there.

ADRIANA
Go back again, thou slave, and fetch him home.

DROMIO OF EPHESUS
Go back again and be new beaten home?
75 For God's sake, send some other messenger.

ADRIANA
Back, slave, or I will break thy pate across.

DROMIO OF EPHESUS
And he will bless that cross with other beating.
Between you, I shall have a holy head.

ADRIANA
Hence, prating peasant! Fetch thy master home.

DROMIO OF EPHESUS
80 Am I so round with you as you with me,
That like a football you do spurn me thus?
You spurn me hence, and he will spurn me hither.
If I last in this service, you must case me in leather.

Exit DROMIO OF EPHESUS

LUCIANA
Fie, how impatience loureth in your face.

"My gold," he said. "Where's the thousand marks I gave you, scoundrel?" "The pig," I said, "is burned." "My gold," he said. "My mistress," I said. "Damn your mistress! I don't know your mistress, the hell with your mistress!"

LUCIANA
Who said that?

DROMIO OF EPHESUS
My master said it. "I don't know," he said, "any house, wife, or mistress." My message, which was supposed to be delivered with my mouth, ended up being carried back home by my shoulders. Because at the end of it all, that's where he beat me.

ADRIANA
Go back again, slave, and bring him home.

DROMIO OF EPHESUS
Go back again, to be beaten home again? For God's sake, send somebody else.

ADRIANA
Go back, slave, or I'll knock you one across the head.

DROMIO OF EPHESUS
And he'll add another knock across. With all these crosses, I'll have a holy head.

ADRIANA
Get out of here, you blathering peasant! Bring your master home.

DROMIO OF EPHESUS
Do I treat you this roundly? You're kicking me around like I'm a football. You kick me out, he kicks me back. If I keep working for you, I'm going to end up wrapped in leather, like a football.

DROMIO OF EPHESUS exits.

LUCIANA
Look at you! You have impatience all over your face.

ADRIANA
85　His company must do his minions grace,
　　Whilst I at home starve for a merry look.
　　Hath homely age th' alluring beauty took
　　From my poor cheek? Then he hath wasted it.
　　Are my discourses dull? Barren my wit?
90　If voluble and sharp discourse be marred,
　　Unkindness blunts it more than marble hard.
　　Do their gay vestments his affections bait?
　　That's not my fault; he's master of my state.
　　What ruins are in me that can be found
95　By him not ruined? Then is he the ground
　　Of my defeatures. My decayèd fair
　　A sunny look of his would soon repair.
　　But, too unruly deer, he breaks the pale
　　And feeds from home. Poor I am but his stale.

LUCIANA
100　Self-harming jealousy, fie, beat it hence.

ADRIANA
　　Unfeeling fools can with such wrongs dispense.
　　I know his eye doth homage otherwhere,
　　Or else what lets it but he would be here?
　　Sister, you know he promised me a chain.
105　Would that alone o' love he would detain,
　　So he would keep fair quarter with his bed.
　　I see the jewel best enamelèd
　　Will lose his beauty. Yet the gold bides still
　　That others touch, and often touching will
110　Wear gold; yet no man that hath a name
　　By falsehood and corruption doth it shame.
　　Since that my beauty cannot please his eye,
　　I'll weep what's left away, and weeping die.

LUCIANA
　　How many fond fools serve mad jealousy!

　　　　　　　　　　　　　　　　　　　　　　　Exeunt

ADRIANA

He feels the need to grace all his other tramps with his presence while I sit at home starving for a smile from him. Has homely old age taken the alluring beauty from my poor cheeks? That's because he has squandered my beauty. Am I boring? Have I lost my wit? If my conversation is no longer free and clever, that's because he's dulled it—I'm like a sharp tool he's blunted with a hard piece of marble. Is he charmed by their pretty clothes? Well, that's not my fault—he's the one in charge of my spending. What faults can you find in me that weren't first caused by him? One smile from him would repair my decayed beauty. But like an unruly deer, he's always trespassing past the park borders and straying away from home to feed in new pastures. I am nothing but a poor, used fool.

LUCIANA

This jealousy is harming only you! Drive it out of you.

ADRIANA

Only someone who doesn't feel this pain could tell me to ignore it. I know his eyes are worshiping some other woman, or why wouldn't he be here? Sister, you know he promised to give me a necklace. I would gladly do without that if he would only stay faithful to me. Even the best jewel can be tarnished. Gold, however, can't be corrupted—though it can be worn down if it's touched too often. And no man with a reputation will tarnish that name with lies and bad behavior. Since my beauty no longer pleases my husband, I'll weep away what's left and then die with weeping.

LUCIANA

How many infatuated people go mad with jealousy!
They exit.

ACT 2, SCENE 2

Enter ANTIPHOLUS OF SYRACUSE

ANTIPHOLUS OF SYRACUSE

The gold I gave to Dromio is laid up
Safe at the Centaur, and the heedful slave
Is wandered forth, in care to seek me out.
By computation and mine host's report,
I could not speak with Dromio since at first
I sent him from the mart. See, here he comes.

Enter DROMIO OF SYRACUSE

How now, sir? is your merry humor altered?
As you love strokes, so jest with me again.
You know no Centaur? You received no gold?
Your mistress sent to have me home to dinner?
My house was at the Phoenix? Wast thou mad,
That thus so madly thou didst answer me?

DROMIO OF SYRACUSE
What answer, sir? When spake I such a word?

ANTIPHOLUS OF SYRACUSE
Even now, even here, not half an hour since.

DROMIO OF SYRACUSE
I did not see you since you sent me hence,
Home to the Centaur with the gold you gave me.

ANTIPHOLUS OF SYRACUSE
Villain, thou didst deny the gold's receipt
And told'st me of a mistress and a dinner,
For which, I hope, thou felt'st I was displeased.

DROMIO OF SYRACUSE
I am glad to see you in this merry vein.
What means this jest? I pray you, master, tell me?

ACT 2, SCENE 2

ANTIPHOLUS OF SYRACUSE *enters.*

ANTIPHOLUS OF SYRACUSE
> The gold I gave Dromio is safe and sound at the Centaur, and the inn host says that Dromio has left and is looking for me. I haven't spoken to him since I sent him away from the marketplace earlier. Here he comes.

DROMIO OF SYRACUSE *enters.*

> So, sir. Are you over your ridiculous mood? If you like being hit, crack some more jokes. You never heard of the Centaur? You weren't given any gold? Your mistress sent for me to come to dinner? The Phoenix is my house? Were you mad when you spoke to me so madly?

DROMIO OF SYRACUSE
> Said what, sir? When did I say all that?

ANTIPHOLUS OF SYRACUSE
> Just now. Right here. Less than half an hour ago.

DROMIO OF SYRACUSE
> I haven't seen you since you sent me to the Centaur with the gold you gave me.

ANTIPHOLUS OF SYRACUSE
> You moron, you denied having any gold, and you told me about a mistress and a lunch. And I hope you realized I wasn't very happy about it.

DROMIO OF SYRACUSE
> I'm glad to see you in such a merry mood. But what's the joke? Please, master, tell me.

ANTIPHOLUS OF SYRACUSE

Yea, dost thou jeer and flout me in the teeth?
Think'st thou I jest? Hold, take thou that and that. *(beats*
DROMIO OF SYRACUSE*)*

DROMIO OF SYRACUSE

Hold, sir, for God's sake! Now your jest is earnest.
25 Upon what bargain do you give it me?

ANTIPHOLUS OF SYRACUSE

Because that I familiarly sometimes
Do use you for my fool and chat with you,
Your sauciness will jest upon my love
And make a common of my serious hours.
30 When the sun shines, let foolish gnats make sport,
But creep in crannies when he hides his beams.
If you will jest with me, know my aspect,
And fashion your demeanor to my looks,
Or I will beat this method in your sconce.

DROMIO OF SYRACUSE

35 "Sconce" call you it? So you would leave battering, I had
rather have it a "head." An you use these blows long, I must
get a sconce for my head and ensconce it too, or else I shall
seek my wit in my shoulders. But I pray, sir, why am I
beaten?

ANTIPHOLUS OF SYRACUSE

40 Dost thou not know?

DROMIO OF SYRACUSE

Nothing, sir, but that I am beaten.

ANTIPHOLUS OF SYRACUSE

Shall I tell you why?

DROMIO OF SYRACUSE

Ay, sir, and wherefore, for they say every why hath a
wherefore.

ANTIPHOLUS OF SYRACUSE

What, are you mocking me to my face? You think I'm joking? Here. Take that, and that! *(beats* DROMIO OF SYRACUSE*)*

DROMIO OF SYRACUSE

Stop, sir, for God's sake! Now this joke has turned serious. Why are you doing this?

ANTIPHOLUS OF SYRACUSE

Just because I act familiar with you sometimes and let you fool around and joke with me, you try to take advantage of my affection. You pull pranks when I'm in a serious mood. You know, foolish gnats come out in the sunshine, but they creep back into their holes when it's dark. If you want to crack jokes, first check what kind of mood I'm in and then adjust your behavior to suit me. If you don't learn this rule, I'll have to beat it into your sconce.

DROMIO OF SYRACUSE

Dromio puns on various meanings of "sconce," including "head," "fortress" (which Dromio imagines being attacked with a battering ram), and "curtain."

You call it my "sconce"? I'd rather call it my "head" so you'd stop battering it. If you keep pounding me, I'll need a sconce to wrap my head with, or else I'll have to keep my brain in my chest. But sir, why are you beating me?

ANTIPHOLUS OF SYRACUSE

Don't you know?

DROMIO OF SYRACUSE

All I know is that I'm being beaten.

ANTIPHOLUS OF SYRACUSE

Should I tell you why?

DROMIO OF SYRACUSE

Yes, and wherefore. You know the old saying: "Every 'why' has a 'wherefore.'"

ANTIPHOLUS OF SYRACUSE

45   "Why" first: for flouting me; and then "wherefore":
        for urging it the second time to me.

DROMIO OF SYRACUSE

        Was there ever any man thus beaten out of season,
        When in the "why" and the "wherefore" is neither rhyme
                nor reason?
        Well, sir, I thank you.

ANTIPHOLUS OF SYRACUSE

50   Thank me, sir, for what?

DROMIO OF SYRACUSE

        Marry, sir, for this something that you gave me for nothing.

ANTIPHOLUS OF SYRACUSE

        I'll make you amends next, to give you nothing for
        something. But say, sir, is it dinnertime?

DROMIO OF SYRACUSE

        No, sir, I think the meat wants that I have.

ANTIPHOLUS OF SYRACUSE

55   In good time, sir, what's that?

DROMIO OF SYRACUSE

        Basting.

ANTIPHOLUS OF SYRACUSE

        Well, sir, then 'twill be dry.

DROMIO OF SYRACUSE

        If it be, sir, I pray you, eat none of it.

ANTIPHOLUS OF SYRACUSE

        Your reason?

DROMIO OF SYRACUSE

60   Lest it make you choleric and purchase me another dry
        basting.

ANTIPHOLUS OF SYRACUSE

        Well, sir, learn to jest in good time. There's a time for all
        things.

DROMIO OF SYRACUSE

        I durst have denied that before you were so choleric.

ANTIPHOLUS OF SYRACUSE

"Why" first: for defying me. And then "wherefore": for doing it a second time.

DROMIO OF SYRACUSE

I don't think any man's ever been beaten for a "why" and "wherefore" that made so little sense. Well, thank you.

ANTIPHOLUS OF SYRACUSE

Thank me? For what?

DROMIO OF SYRACUSE

Because you gave me something for nothing.

ANTIPHOLUS OF SYRACUSE

Next time I'll give you nothing for something. Is it lunchtime?

DROMIO OF SYRACUSE

No. The meat lacks something that I have.

ANTIPHOLUS OF SYRACUSE

What would that be?

DROMIO OF SYRACUSE

A basting.

ANTIPHOLUS OF SYRACUSE

Well, then it will be dry.

DROMIO OF SYRACUSE

If it is, I suggest you don't eat it.

ANTIPHOLUS OF SYRACUSE

Why not?

DROMIO OF SYRACUSE

Because it will make you angry, and that will get me another beating.

ANTIPHOLUS OF SYRACUSE

Well, learn to make jokes at the appropriate time. There's a time for all things.

DROMIO OF SYRACUSE

Before you got so angry, I never would have thought that.

ANTIPHOLUS OF SYRACUSE
65   By what rule, sir?

DROMIO OF SYRACUSE
Marry, sir, by a rule as plain as the plain bald pate of Father Time himself.

ANTIPHOLUS OF SYRACUSE
Let's hear it.

DROMIO OF SYRACUSE
70   There's no time for a man to recover his hair that grows bald by nature.

ANTIPHOLUS OF SYRACUSE
May he not do it by fine and recovery?

DROMIO OF SYRACUSE
Yes, to pay a fine for a periwig, and recover the lost hair of another man.

ANTIPHOLUS OF SYRACUSE
75   Why is Time such a niggard of hair, being, as it is, so plentiful an excrement?

DROMIO OF SYRACUSE
Because it is a blessing that he bestows on beasts, and what he hath scanted men in hair, he hath given them in wit.

ANTIPHOLUS OF SYRACUSE
Why, but there's many a man hath more hair than wit.

DROMIO OF SYRACUSE
80   Not a man of those but he hath the wit to lose his hair.

ANTIPHOLUS OF SYRACUSE
Why, thou didst conclude hairy men plain dealers without wit.

ANTIPHOLUS OF SYRACUSE
Why not?

DROMIO OF SYRACUSE
I'll tell you: it's because of a law as plain as Father Time's bald head.

ANTIPHOLUS OF SYRACUSE
Let's hear it.

DROMIO OF SYRACUSE
There may be a time for everything, but no man who has gone bald naturally can get his hair back.

ANTIPHOLUS OF SYRACUSE
Can't he get it by fine and recovery?

Fine and recovery = a legal term related to claiming ownership of private property

DROMIO OF SYRACUSE
Yes, he can pay a fine for a wig and then recover another man's lost hair.

ANTIPHOLUS OF SYRACUSE
Why is Time so cheap about giving out hair? After all, it's plentiful in its growth.

DROMIO OF SYRACUSE
Because animals are blessed with hair. With men, he's been stingy with hair, but he makes up for it by giving them intelligence.

ANTIPHOLUS OF SYRACUSE
But a lot of men have more hair than intelligence.

DROMIO OF SYRACUSE
And not one of them is smart enough to stop himself from going bald.

ANTIPHOLUS OF SYRACUSE
So then, you must think that hairy men are honest and simpleminded.

DROMIO OF SYRACUSE
The plainer dealer, the sooner lost. Yet he loseth it in a kind
of jollity.

ANTIPHOLUS OF SYRACUSE
85   For what reason?

DROMIO OF SYRACUSE
For two, and sound ones too.

ANTIPHOLUS OF SYRACUSE
Nay, not sound, I pray you.

DROMIO OF SYRACUSE
Sure ones, then.

ANTIPHOLUS OF SYRACUSE
Nay, not sure, in a thing falsing.

DROMIO OF SYRACUSE
90   Certain ones, then.

ANTIPHOLUS OF SYRACUSE
Name them.

DROMIO OF SYRACUSE
The one, to save the money that he spends in tiring; the
other, that at dinner they should not drop in his porridge.

ANTIPHOLUS OF SYRACUSE
You would all this time have proved there is no time for all
95   things.

DROMIO OF SYRACUSE
Marry, and did, sir: namely, e'en no time to recover hair lost
by nature.

DROMIO OF SYRACUSE

In the original Shakespearean line, there are a series of sexual puns and jokes about venereal diseases–venereal disease can cause hair loss; "sound" can mean "healthy," "thing" can refer to a sexual organ, and "falsing" means "deceptive."

The more simpleminded they are, the sooner they lose their hair. But they have a good time doing so.

ANTIPHOLUS OF SYRACUSE

Why?

DROMIO OF SYRACUSE

Two reasons. And good ones, too.

ANTIPHOLUS OF SYRACUSE

Not good ones, please.

DROMIO OF SYRACUSE

Then sure ones.

ANTIPHOLUS OF SYRACUSE

No, not sure ones when we're talking about something unsure.

DROMIO OF SYRACUSE

Then certain ones.

ANTIPHOLUS OF SYRACUSE

Name them.

DROMIO OF SYRACUSE

One, so they can save the money they spent on hairstyling, and two, so that when their hair falls out it doesn't land in their dinner.

ANTIPHOLUS OF SYRACUSE

You were supposed to be proving that there isn't time for everything.

DROMIO OF SYRACUSE

Right, and I did, sir. There's no time to get back hair that's fallen out.

ANTIPHOLUS OF SYRACUSE

But your reason was not substantial why there is no time to recover.

DROMIO OF SYRACUSE

100   Thus I mend it: Time himself is bald and therefore, to the world's end, will have bald followers.

ANTIPHOLUS OF SYRACUSE

I knew 'twould be a bald conclusion:
But soft, who wafts us yonder?

Enter ADRIANA *and* LUCIANA

ADRIANA

Ay, ay, Antipholus, look strange and frown.
105   Some other mistress hath thy sweet aspects.
I am not Adriana, nor thy wife.
The time was once when thou unurged wouldst vow
That never words were music to thine ear,
That never object pleasing in thine eye,
110   That never touch well welcome to thy hand,
That never meat sweet-savored in thy taste,
Unless I spake, or looked, or touched, or carved to thee.
How comes it now, my husband, O, how comes it
That thou art thus estranged from thyself?
115   "Thyself" I call it, being strange to me,
That, undividable, incorporate,
Am better than thy dear self's better part.
Ah, do not tear away thyself from me!
For know, my love, as easy mayest thou fall
120   A drop of water in the breaking gulf,
And take unmingled thence that drop again
Without addition or diminishing,
As take from me thyself and not me too.
How dearly would it touch thee to the quick,
125   Shouldst thou but hear I were licentious
And that this body, consecrate to thee,

ANTIPHOLUS OF SYRACUSE

You didn't come up with a very good proof.

DROMIO OF SYRACUSE

Then I'll change it to this: Father Time himself is bald, so for all time there will be bald men.

ANTIPHOLUS OF SYRACUSE

I knew you'd come up with a bald conclusion. But wait—who's that waving to us?

"Bald" can also mean "trivial" or "lame."

ADRIANA *and* LUCIANA *enter.*

ADRIANA

Yes, yes, Antipholus: look bewildered and frown at me. You've given away all your sweet looks to some other woman—I am not Adriana nor your wife. There was a time when you'd freely tell me that words were never music to your ear unless I said them, that objects never pleased your eye unless I showed them to you, that touches never pleased your hands unless they were my touches, and that food never tasted sweet to you unless I had prepared it. How is it, my husband— oh, how is it—that you have become a stranger to yourself? I say yourself because you are a stranger to me now, but when we are indivisible and united in one body, I am better than the best part of you. Ah, don't tear yourself away from me! For you should know, my love, that it would be as easy to let a drop of water fall into the churning sea and then fish it out again, unmingled and undiminished, as it would be to take yourself from me without taking me out of myself as well. How deeply would it cut you if you heard that I had been cheating on you and that my body—which is sworn for you only—had been contaminated by vile lust?

By ruffian lust should be contaminate!
Wouldst thou not spit at me, and spurn at me,
And hurl the name of husband in my face,
130 And tear the stained skin off my harlot brow,
And from my false hand cut the wedding ring,
And break it with a deep-divorcing vow?
I know thou canst, and therefore see thou do it.
I am possessed with an adulterate blot;
135 My blood is mingled with the crime of lust;
For if we too be one, and thou play false,
I do digest the poison of thy flesh,
Being strumpeted by thy contagion.
Keep then fair league and truce with thy true bed,
140 I live disstained, thou undishonorèd.

ANTIPHOLUS OF SYRACUSE
Plead you to me, fair dame? I know you not.
In Ephesus I am but two hours old,
As strange unto your town as to your talk,
Who, every word by all my wit being scanned,
145 Want wit in all one word to understand.

LUCIANA
Fie, brother, how the world is changed with you!
When were you wont to use my sister thus?
She sent for you by Dromio home to dinner.

ANTIPHOLUS OF SYRACUSE
By Dromio?

DROMIO OF SYRACUSE
150 By me?

ADRIANA
By thee; and this thou didst return from him:
That he did buffet thee and, in his blows,
Denied my house for his, me for his wife.

ANTIPHOLUS OF SYRACUSE
Did you converse, sir, with this gentlewoman?
155 What is the course and drift of your compact?

Wouldn't you spit at me, and spurn me, and throw our marriage vows in my face? Wouldn't you tear the mark off my whorish forehead, cut the wedding ring off my finger, and swear to divorce me? I know you would, so go ahead. For I have, in fact, committed adultery, and my blood has been contaminated by lust. Because if marriage has made us one, then when you cheat, you poison my flesh as well—your contagion makes me a prostitute. So stay faithful to me and return to your marriage bed. That way, my reputation will be protected and your honor will be intact.

Whores were commonly punished by being branded on the forehead.

ANTIPHOLUS OF SYRACUSE

Are you talking to me, fair woman? I don't know you. I've only been in Ephesus for two hours. Your talk is as strange to me as your town. I'm trying with all my wits to figure out what you mean, but I can't understand a word of it.

LUCIANA

Shame on you, brother-in-law! You've changed so much! Why are you treating my sister like this? She sent Dromio to bring you home for lunch.

ANTIPHOLUS OF SYRACUSE
Dromio?

DROMIO OF SYRACUSE
Me?

ADRIANA

You. And this is what you told me he said: that he beat you and pretended his house wasn't his and I wasn't his wife.

ANTIPHOLUS OF SYRACUSE

Did you talk with this woman? What kind of scheme do you have going together?

DROMIO OF SYRACUSE

    I, sir? I never saw her till this time.

ANTIPHOLUS OF SYRACUSE

    Villain, thou liest; for even her very words

    Didst thou deliver to me on the mart.

DROMIO OF SYRACUSE

160   I never spake with her in all my life.

ANTIPHOLUS OF SYRACUSE

    How can she thus then call us by our names—

    Unless it be by inspiration?

ADRIANA

    How ill agrees it with your gravity

165   To counterfeit thus grossly with your slave,

    Abetting him to thwart me in my mood.

    Be it my wrong you are from me exempt,

    But wrong not that wrong with a more contempt.

    Come, I will fasten on this sleeve of thine.

170   Thou art an elm, my husband, I a vine,

    Whose weakness, married to thy stronger state,

    Makes me with thy strength to communicate.

    If aught possess thee from me, it is dross,

    Usurping ivy, brier, or idle moss,

    Who, all for want of pruning, with intrusion

175   Infect thy sap and live on thy confusion.

ANTIPHOLUS OF SYRACUSE

    To me she speaks; she moves me for her theme.

    What, was I married to her in my dream?

    Or sleep I now and think I hear all this?

180   What error drives our eyes and ears amiss?

    Until I know this sure uncertainty

    I'll entertain the offered fallacy.

LUCIANA

    Dromio, go bid the servants spread for dinner.

DROMIO OF SYRACUSE

    O, for my beads! I cross me for a sinner.

185   This is the fairy land. O spite of spites!

DROMIO OF SYRACUSE
Me, sir? I never saw her till now.

ANTIPHOLUS OF SYRACUSE
You liar! You said those exact things to me back in the marketplace.

DROMIO OF SYRACUSE
I never talked with her in my life.

ANTIPHOLUS OF SYRACUSE
Then how does she know our names? By magic?

ADRIANA
How distasteful! That a man of your stature would scheme with his servant to upset me like this. It may be my fault that you've been avoiding me, but don't make things worse by treating me with contempt as well. I'll hang on your sleeve: you're an elm tree, my husband, and I'm a vine. My weakness is enhanced by your strength, which gives me the strength to say this: the things that take you away from me are worthless—just overgrown weeds in need of a trimming. They get into your system and infect you, feeding off your confusion.

ANTIPHOLUS OF SYRACUSE
She's talking to me. She's talking about me. What, was I married to her in a dream? Or am I asleep now and imagining all this? What is making our eyes and ears act so strangely? Until I know for sure, I'll humor her.

LUCIANA
Dromio, tell the servants to prepare for lunch.

DROMIO OF SYRACUSE
Oh, I wish I had my rosary! I'll cross myself. This must be some kind of fairyland. Oh, spite of spites!

We talk with goblins, owls, and sprites:
If we obey them not, this will ensue:
They'll suck our breath, or pinch us black and blue.

LUCIANA
190 Why prat'st thou to thyself and answer'st not?
Dromio—thou, Dromio—thou snail, thou slug, thou sot.

DROMIO OF SYRACUSE
I am transformèd, master, am I not?

ANTIPHOLUS OF SYRACUSE
I think thou art in mind, and so am I.

DROMIO OF SYRACUSE
Nay, master, both in mind and in my shape.

ANTIPHOLUS OF SYRACUSE
195 Thou hast thine own form.

DROMIO OF SYRACUSE
                                                No, I am an ape.

LUCIANA
If thou art changed to aught, 'tis to an ass.

DROMIO OF SYRACUSE
'Tis true. She rides me, and I long for grass.
'Tis so. I am an ass; else it could never be
But I should know her as well as she knows me.

ADRIANA
200 Come, come, no longer will I be a fool,
To put the finger in the eye and weep
Whilst man and master laugh my woes to scorn.
Come, sir, to dinner.—Dromio, keep the gate. —
Husband, I'll dine above with you today,
205 And shrive you of a thousand idle pranks.
Sirrah, if any ask you for your master,
Say he dines forth, and let no creature enter.—
Come, sister.—Dromio, play the porter well.

ANTIPHOLUS OF SYRACUSE
Am I in earth, in heaven, or in hell?
210 Sleeping or waking, mad or well-advised?

We're speaking with goblins, owls, and demons. If we don't obey them, they'll suck the life out of us or pinch us black and blue.

LUCIANA

Why are you mumbling to yourself instead of answering the order I gave you? Dromio, you drone, you snail, you slug, you idiot!

DROMIO OF SYRACUSE

I've been transformed somehow, haven't I, master?

ANTIPHOLUS OF SYRACUSE

I think your mind has been altered, and mine too.

DROMIO OF SYRACUSE

No, master, I've been changed in both mind and body.

ANTIPHOLUS OF SYRACUSE

Your body looks the same.

DROMIO OF SYRACUSE

No, I'm an ape.

ape = a counterfeit (of myself); a fool

LUCIANA

If you've changed into anything, it's an ass.

DROMIO OF SYRACUSE

That's true. She's riding me hard, and all I want to do is get out of here. I must be as stupid as an ass—that's why I don't know her, but she knows me.

ADRIANA

All right, all right. I won't play the fool anymore and just cry while my husband and his man laugh at me. Come, husband, let's go to lunch. Dromio, guard the door. Husband, I'll eat with you in private today and hear your confession about all the pranks you've pulled. Sirrah, if anyone asks where your master is, say he's out to lunch, and don't let anyone come in. Come, sister. Dromio, do a good job as doorkeeper.

Sirrah = term of address for a person of low social standing

ANTIPHOLUS OF SYRACUSE

Am I on earth, in heaven, or in hell? Asleep or awake? Crazy or sane? These people know me, but I don't

Known unto these, and to myself disguised!
I'll say as they say, and persever so,
And in this mist at all adventures go.

DROMIO OF SYRACUSE
Master, shall I be porter at the gate?

ADRIANA
215   Ay; and let none enter, lest I break your pate.

LUCIANA
Come, come, Antipholus, we dine too late.

Exeunt

know myself! I'll agree with them and keep with it,
whatever happens.

DROMIO OF SYRACUSE

Master, should I watch the door?

ADRIANA

Yes, and don't let anyone come in, or else I'll break
your head.

LUCIANA

Come come, Antipholus. We're late for lunch.

They exit.

ACT THREE

SCENE 1

Enter ANTIPHOLUS OF EPHESUS, DROMIO OF EPHESUS,
ANGELO, *and* BALTHASAR

ANTIPHOLUS OF EPHESUS
Good Signior Angelo, you must excuse us all;
My wife is shrewish when I keep not hours.
Say that I lingered with you at your shop
To see the making of her carcanet,
5 And that tomorrow you will bring it home.
But here's a villain that would face me down
He met me on the mart, and that I beat him
And charged him with a thousand marks in gold,
And that I did deny my wife and house.—
10 Thou drunkard, thou, what didst thou mean by this?

DROMIO OF EPHESUS
Say what you will, sir, but I know what I know.
That you beat me at the mart I have your hand to show;
If the skin were parchment and the blows you gave were ink,
Your own handwriting would tell you what I think.

ANTIPHOLUS OF EPHESUS
15 I think thou art an ass.

DROMIO OF EPHESUS
⠀⠀⠀⠀⠀⠀⠀⠀⠀⠀Marry, so it doth appear
By the wrongs I suffer and the blows I bear.
I should kick being kicked; and, being at that pass,
You would keep from my heels and beware of an ass.

ANTIPHOLUS OF EPHESUS
You're sad, Signior Balthasar. Pray God our cheer
20 May answer my good will and your good welcome here.

ACT THREE

SCENE 1

ANTIPHOLUS OF EPHESUS, DROMIO OF EPHESUS,
ANGELO, *and* BALTHASAR *enter.*

ANTIPHOLUS OF EPHESUS
Signior Angelo, please excuse us. My wife gets angry
when I'm late. Here's the story we'll tell her: that I was
with you at your shop, watching you make her necklace, and that you're going to deliver it tomorrow. But
here comes a scoundrel who says he saw me at the marketplace and that I beat on him, told him I'd given him
a thousand marks in gold, and then lied about my wife
and my house. You drunkard, what was that all about?

DROMIO OF EPHESUS
Say what you want, but I know what I know. You beat
me at the marketplace, and I have the bruises to prove
it. If my skin were paper and your punches were ink,
you could read the beating on my body.

ANTIPHOLUS OF EPHESUS
I think you're an ass.

DROMIO OF EPHESUS
Honestly, it sure looks that way, judging by all the
beatings and the bad treatment I'm getting. Since I'm
an ass, I ought to kick like one. Then you'd be scared
of me and keep away.

ANTIPHOLUS OF EPHESUS
Signior Balthasar, you look upset. I hope the good
meal I'm going to give you will show the goodwill I
bear you and how welcome you are.

BALTHASAR
> I hold your dainties cheap, sir, and your welcome dear.

ANTIPHOLUS OF EPHESUS
> O Signior Balthasar, either at flesh or fish
> A table full of welcome make scarce one dainty dish.

BALTHASAR
> Good meat, sir, is common; that every churl affords.

ANTIPHOLUS OF EPHESUS
25
> And welcome more common, for that's nothing but words.

BALTHASAR
> Small cheer and great welcome makes a merry feast.

ANTIPHOLUS OF EPHESUS
> Ay, to a niggardly host and more sparing guest.
> But though my cates be mean, take them in good part.
> Better cheer may you have, but not with better heart.
30
> But soft! My door is lock'd. *(to* DROMIO*)* Go, bid them let
> us in.

DROMIO OF EPHESUS
> Maud, Bridget, Marian, Ciceley, Gillian, Ginn!

DROMIO OF SYRACUSE
> *(within)* Mome, malt-horse, capon, coxcomb, idiot, patch!
> Either get thee from the door or sit down at the hatch.
> Dost thou conjure for wenches, that thou call'st for
> such store
35
> When one is one too many? Go, get thee from the door.

DROMIO OF EPHESUS
> What patch is made our porter? My master stays in
> the street.

DROMIO OF SYRACUSE
> *(within)* Let him walk from whence he came, lest he catch
> cold on 's feet.

ANTIPHOLUS OF EPHESUS
> Who talks within there? Ho, open the door.

BALTHASAR

Your delicacies aren't worth as much to me as your welcome is.

ANTIPHOLUS OF EPHESUS

Signior Balthasar, all the welcome in the world can't compare to a good meal, whatever kind of food it might be.

BALTHASAR

Good food's not a big deal—everyone can afford that.

ANTIPHOLUS OF EPHESUS

And everyone can say "welcome," which is just a word.

BALTHASAR

A little food and a huge welcome makes a joyous feast.

ANTIPHOLUS OF EPHESUS

Sure, to a cheap host and an even cheaper guest. But look, even if my dishes are poor, eat them with my best wishes. You may come across better food, but not a warmer welcome. What's this? My door is locked. *(to* DROMIO*)* Tell them to let us in.

DROMIO OF EPHESUS

Maud, Bridget, Marian, Ciceley, Gillian, Ginn!

DROMIO OF SYRACUSE

(from offstage) Dope, moron, eunuch, fool, idiot, clown! Either get away from the door or sit yourself down there! What, are you trying to summon women with your spells—is that why you're calling out so many names? Isn't one enough for you? Get away with you!

DROMIO OF EPHESUS

What clown did they hire as the new doorkeeper? My master is standing out in the street!

DROMIO OF SYRACUSE

(from offstage) Then he should go back where he came from so he doesn't catch a cold.

ANTIPHOLUS OF EPHESUS

Who's in there? Hey, open the door!

DROMIO OF SYRACUSE
> *(within)* Right, sir, I'll tell you when an you tell me
> wherefore.

ANTIPHOLUS OF EPHESUS
40   Wherefore? For my dinner. I have not dined today.

DROMIO OF SYRACUSE
> *(within)* Nor today here you must not. Come again when
> you may.

ANTIPHOLUS OF EPHESUS
> What art thou that keep'st me out from the house I owe?

DROMIO OF SYRACUSE
> *(within)* The porter for this time, sir, and my name is
> Dromio.

DROMIO OF EPHESUS
> O villain, thou hast stolen both mine office and my name!
45   The one ne'er got me credit, the other mickle blame.
> If thou hadst been Dromio today in my place,
> Thou wouldst have changed thy face for a name, or thy
> name for an ass.

LUCE
> *(within)* What a coil is there, Dromio! Who are those at the
> gate?

DROMIO OF EPHESUS
> Let my master in, Luce.

LUCE
>   *(within)* Faith, no, he comes too late,
50   And so tell your master.

DROMIO OF EPHESUS
>   O Lord, I must laugh.
> Have at you with a proverb: shall I set in my staff?

LUCE
> *(within)* Have at you with another: that's—When, can
> you tell?

DROMIO OF SYRACUSE

(from offstage) Right. Give me one good reason and I will.

ANTIPHOLUS OF EPHESUS

A reason? So I can eat lunch. I haven't eaten today.

DROMIO OF SYRACUSE

(from offstage) And you won't eat here today. Come again some other time.

ANTIPHOLUS OF EPHESUS

Who do you think you are, keeping me out of my own house?

DROMIO OF SYRACUSE

(from offstage) I'm the doorkeeper for the moment, and my name is Dromio.

DROMIO OF EPHESUS

You jerk! You've stolen both my job and my name! True, the job never did me much good, and my name only ever got me in trouble. If you were the Dromio in my shoes today, you would have felt like you traded your head for a target and your name for the name of "Ass."

LUCE

In a later printing of the play, the character of Luce was renamed "Nell."

(from offstage) What's all the commotion, Dromio? Who's at the door?

DROMIO OF EPHESUS

Luce, let my master in.

LUCE

(from offstage) No way, he's too late. Tell your master that.

DROMIO OF EPHESUS

Oh, Lord, this makes me laugh! I'll come at you with the old proverb: "Should I make myself at home?"

LUCE

(from offstage) I'll come at you with another: "I'd like to see you try it!"

DROMIO OF SYRACUSE
> *(within)* If thy name be called "Luce," Luce, thou hast answered him well.

ANTIPHOLUS OF EPHESUS
> Do you hear, you minion? You'll let us in, I hope?

LUCE
55   *(within)* I thought to have asked you.

DROMIO OF SYRACUSE
>   *(within)* And you said no.

DROMIO OF EPHESUS
> So, come, help. Well struck! There was blow for blow.

ANTIPHOLUS OF EPHESUS
> Thou baggage, let me in.

LUCE
>   *(within)* Can you tell for whose sake?

DROMIO OF EPHESUS
> Master, knock the door hard.

LUCE
>   *(within)* Let him knock till it ache.

ANTIPHOLUS OF EPHESUS
> You'll cry for this, minion, if I beat the door down.

LUCE
60   *(within)* What needs all that, and a pair of stocks in the town?

ADRIANA
> *(within)* Who is that at the door that keeps all this noise?

DROMIO OF SYRACUSE
> *(within)* By my troth, your town is troubled with unruly boys.

DROMIO OF SYRACUSE

(from offstage) If your name's Luce, then I say: Luce, good answer!

ANTIPHOLUS OF EPHESUS

Listen up, you slave. Are you going to let us in?

LUCE

(from offstage) I was going to ask you that question.

DROMIO OF SYRACUSE

(from offstage) But you already answered no.

DROMIO OF EPHESUS

Come, help me bang on the door, master. Well done! We answered them, blow for blow.

ANTIPHOLUS OF EPHESUS

You good-for-nothing, let me in.

LUCE

(from offstage) Says who?

DROMIO OF EPHESUS

Master, knock hard upon the door.

LUCE

(from offstage) He can knock till it hurts.

ANTIPHOLUS OF EPHESUS

If I break the door down, slave, you'll be sorry for this.

LUCE

stocks = an instrument of public punishment. Offenders had their hands and feet locked in a wooden frame and were left to be mocked and abused.

(from offstage) Why are we putting up with all this? The town's got a pair of stocks.

ADRIANA

(from offstage) Who's making such a ruckus at the door?

DROMIO OF SYRACUSE

(from offstage) I swear, this town's plagued by troublesome boys.

ANTIPHOLUS OF EPHESUS
> Are you there, wife? You might have come before.

ADRIANA
> *(within)* Your wife, sir knave? Go, get you from the door.

DROMIO OF EPHESUS
65
> If you went in pain, master, this knave would go sore.

ANGELO
> Here is neither cheer, sir, nor welcome. We would fain
>> have either.

BALTHASAR
> In debating which was best, we shall part with neither.

DROMIO OF EPHESUS
> They stand at the door, master. Bid them welcome hither.

ANTIPHOLUS OF EPHESUS
> There is something in the wind, that we cannot get in.

DROMIO OF EPHESUS
70
> You would say so, master, if your garments were thin.
> Your cake there is warm within; you stand here in the cold.
> It would make a man mad as a buck to be so bought and sold.

ANTIPHOLUS OF EPHESUS
> Go, fetch me something: I'll break ope the gate.

DROMIO OF SYRACUSE
> *(within)* Break any breaking here, and I'll break your
>> knave's pate.

DROMIO OF EPHESUS
75
> A man may break a word with you, sir, and words are
>> but wind,
> Ay, and break it in your face, so he break it not behind.

DROMIO OF SYRACUSE
> *(within)* It seems thou want'st breaking. Out upon thee,
>> hind!

ANTIPHOLUS OF EPHESUS

Is that you, wife? You could have come sooner.

ADRIANA

(from offstage) Your wife, you scoundrel? Get away from the door.

DROMIO OF EPHESUS

If she punishes you, master, she's sure to punish me.

ANGELO

It looks like we're not going to get food or welcome here.

BALTHASAR

We argued about which was best, and now we won't get either one.

DROMIO OF EPHESUS

Master, your guests are just standing here. Tell them they're welcome.

ANTIPHOLUS OF EPHESUS

There's something strange in the air that's keeping us from getting in.

DROMIO OF EPHESUS

And if your clothes were as thin as mine, you'd really feel the air. The food inside is warm, but you're out here freezing. It would make any man as mad as a bull to be betrayed like this.

ANTIPHOLUS OF EPHESUS

Go get me something I can use to break down the door.

DROMIO OF SYRACUSE

(from offstage) Break anything here and I'll break your head.

DROMIO OF EPHESUS

I'll break words with you, sir. And since words are just wind, I'll be breaking wind right in your face.

DROMIO OF SYRACUSE

(from offstage) It seems you're the one who needs to be broken. Be off with you, you dog!

DROMIO OF EPHESUS
> Here's too much "out upon thee!" I pray thee, let me in.

DROMIO OF SYRACUSE
> *(within)* Ay, when fowls have no feathers and fish have
>   no fin.

ANTIPHOLUS OF EPHESUS
80   Well, I'll break in. Go, borrow me a crow.

DROMIO OF EPHESUS
> A crow without feather? Master, mean you so?
> For a fish without a fin, there's a fowl without a feather.—
> *(to* DROMIO OF SYRACUSE*)* If a crow help us in, sirrah, we'll
>   pluck a crow together.

ANTIPHOLUS OF EPHESUS
> Go, get thee gone. Fetch me an iron crow.

BALTHASAR
85   Have patience, sir. O, let it not be so.
> Herein you war against your reputation,
> And draw within the compass of suspect
> Th' unviolated honor of your wife.
> Once this: your long experience of her wisdom,
90   Her sober virtue, years, and modesty
> Plead on her part some cause to you unknown.
> And doubt not, sir, but she will well excuse
> Why at this time the doors are made against you.
> Be ruled by me; depart in patience,
95   And let us to the Tiger all to dinner,
> And about evening come yourself alone
> To know the reason of this strange restraint.
> If by strong hand you offer to break in
> Now in the stirring passage of the day,
100 A vulgar comment will be made of it;
> And that supposèd by the common rout
> Against your yet ungallèd estimation
> That may with foul intrusion enter in

DROMIO OF EPHESUS

I've had enough of this "off with you!" Come on, let me in!

DROMIO OF SYRACUSE

(from offstage) Of course—when birds have no feathers and fish have no fins.

ANTIPHOLUS OF EPHESUS

Well, I'm going to break in. Go get me a crow.

DROMIO OF EPHESUS

A crow without feathers? Master, do you really mean that? He said "when fish have no fins," and you came back with a bird with no feathers. *(to* DROMIO OF SYRACUSE*)* If a crow gets us in, sirrah, then you and I will have a crow to pluck together.

"crow to pluck together" = score to settle with each other

→

ANTIPHOLUS OF EPHESUS

I meant a crowbar. Get going already.

BALTHASAR

Be patient, sir! Don't do this! This will hurt your reputation and make your wife, who's innocent, look suspicious. Look, you've known her a long time. She's wise, serious, mature, and modest. All this suggests that she has a good reason for doing this to you. Let's assume that she has a reason, which you don't know yet: have faith that she'll eventually explain why she shut the doors on you today. Listen to me. Be patient and leave, and we'll all go to the Tiger for lunch. In the evening, come back alone and figure out this strange resistance. If you get violent and break in now, in broad daylight, people will talk about it. The common mob will presume things, and your untarnished reputation will be damaged—and that damage will last long after you're dead. Slander passes from generation to generation, and once it sticks to a family, it's there forever.

And dwell upon your grave when you are dead;
105 For slander lives upon succession,
Forever housèd where it gets possession.

ANTIPHOLUS OF EPHESUS
You have prevailed. I will depart in quiet
And, in despite of mirth, mean to be merry.
I know a wench of excellent discourse,
110 Pretty and witty, wild and yet, too, gentle.
There will we dine. This woman that I mean,
My wife—but, I protest, without desert—
Hath oftentimes upbraided me withal;
To her will we to dinner. *(to* ANGELO*)* Get you home
115 And fetch the chain; by this I know 'tis made.
Bring it, I pray you, to the Porpentine,
For there's the house. That chain will I bestow—
Be it for nothing but to spite my wife—
Upon mine hostess there. Good sir, make haste.
120 Since mine own doors refuse to entertain me,
I'll knock elsewhere, to see if they'll disdain me.

ANGELO
I'll meet you at that place some hour hence.

ANTIPHOLUS OF EPHESUS
Do so. This jest shall cost me some expense.

Exeunt

ANTIPHOLUS OF EPHESUS

You're right—I'll go quietly. And even though I'm in a distasteful mood, I'll work on being happy. I know a terrific wench. She's beautiful and charming—a little wild, but also gentle. We'll eat at her place. My wife has accused me more than once of misbehaving with this woman. I swear to her that I haven't, but it doesn't change anything. We'll go to her place for lunch. *(to* ANGELO*)* Go get the necklace, which I'm sure is done by now. Bring it to the Porcupine, where this woman is. I'll to give it to her, just to spite my wife. Hurry, good sir. Since my own doors refuse to admit me, I'll knock somewhere else and see if they turn me away as well.

ANGELO

I'll meet you there in an hour.

ANTIPHOLUS OF EPHESUS

Do that. This little prank of hers is going to cost me.

They exit.

ACT 3, SCENE 2

Enter LUCIANA *and* ANTIPHOLUS OF SYRACUSE

LUCIANA
And may it be that you have quite forgot
A husband's office? Shall, Antipholus,
Even in the spring of love thy love-springs rot?
Shall love, in building, grow so ruinous?
5 If you did wed my sister for her wealth,
Then for her wealth's sake use her with more kindness.
Or if you like elsewhere, do it by stealth—
Muffle your false love with some show of blindness.
Let not my sister read it in your eye;
10 Be not thy tongue thy own shame's orator;
Look sweet, be fair, become disloyalty;
Apparel vice like virtue's harbinger.
Bear a fair presence, though your heart be tainted.
Teach sin the carriage of a holy saint.
15 Be secret-false. What need she be acquainted?
What simple thief brags of his own attaint?
'Tis double wrong to truant with your bed
And let her read it in thy looks at board.
Shame hath a bastard fame, well managèd;
20 Ill deeds is doubled with an evil word.
Alas, poor women, make us but believe,
Being compact of credit, that you love us.
Though others have the arm, show us the sleeve;
We in your motion turn, and you may move us.
25 Then, gentle brother, get you in again.
Comfort my sister, cheer her, call her wife.
'Tis holy sport to be a little vain
When the sweet breath of flattery conquers strife.

ANTIPHOLUS OF SYRACUSE
Sweet mistress—what your name is else I know not,
30 Nor by what wonder you do hit of mine,—

ACT 3, SCENE 2

LUCIANA *and* ANTIPHOLUS OF SYRACUSE *enter.*

LUCIANA

Have you completely forgotten your duty as a husband? Antipholus, your marriage is still fresh and new, like the springtime—have the young shoots of your love already started to wither? Is the building of your love already in ruins? If you married my sister for her wealth, then for her wealth's sake, treat her with more kindness. Or if your affection has already strayed to another woman, at least be stealthy about it. Hide your false love, blindfold yourself so my sister cannot read your faithlessness in your eyes. Watch what you say, and don't let your own words give away your shame. Look sweet and act kindly—be attractive in your disloyalty. Disguise your misbehavior as integrity, and behave properly even if your heart is tainted. Though you are sinful, carry yourself like a holy saint. Be false in secret: why does she need to know? What foolish thief brags about his crimes? It's doubly wrong to cheat on your wife and then let her see the offense in your eyes. When you do something shameful, it's possible to put a good spin on it, but bad deeds are made worse by speaking of them. Alas, poor women! We're so gullible, we believe it when you say you love us. Even if you love someone else in your heart, make it appear as if you love us. We follow in your orbit, and you have the power to move us. So, my sweet brother-in-law, go inside. Comfort my sister, cheer her up, call her "wife." It's a holy thing to lie a little when sweet flattery can smooth over trouble.

ANTIPHOLUS OF SYRACUSE

Sweet mistress—I don't know what other name to give you, or how you've figured out mine—you seem

Less in your knowledge and your grace you show not
Than our earth's wonder, more than earth divine.
Teach me, dear creature, how to think and speak.
Lay open to my earthy gross conceit,
35   Smothered in errors, feeble, shallow, weak,
The folded meaning of your words' deceit.
Against my soul's pure truth why labour you
To make it wander in an unknown field?
Are you a god? would you create me new?
40   Transform me, then, and to your power I'll yield.
But if that I am I, then well I know
Your weeping sister is no wife of mine,
Nor to her bed no homage do I owe.
Far more, far more, to you do I decline.
45   O, train me not, sweet mermaid, with thy note
To drown me in thy sister's flood of tears.
Sing, Siren, for thyself, and I will dote.
Spread o'er the silver waves thy golden hairs,
And as a bed I'll take them and there lie,
50   And in that glorious supposition think
He gains by death that hath such means to die.
Let Love, being light, be drownèd if she sink.

LUCIANA
What, are you mad that you do reason so?

ANTIPHOLUS OF SYRACUSE
Not mad, but mated—how, I do not know.

LUCIANA
55   It is a fault that springeth from your eye.

ANTIPHOLUS OF SYRACUSE
For gazing on your beams, fair sun, being by.

as wise and graceful as the earth is wonderful and divine. Teach me how I should think and speak. My understanding is clumsy and human, riddled with errors—it is feeble, shallow, and weak. Reveal to me the hidden meaning of your words. Why would you have me betray the truth of my emotions and make my love wander in some other direction? Are you a god? Are you trying to remake me? Go ahead, I'll yield to your power. But if I am myself, then I know for sure that your weeping sister is not my wife. I don't owe her any duty—it's you that I submit to. Oh, sweet mermaid, don't command me to drown myself in the flood of your sister's tears. Siren, use your song to make me love you instead, and I will obey. Spread your golden hair over the silver waves, and I will lie down in it like a bed. If a man could die in that glorious fantasy, then I think he would benefit by dying. Love is light and therefore floats—if my love is false, let me sink!

sirens = mermaids of Greek myth who lured men to their death with their singing

"To die" also has the suggestion "to orgasm."

LUCIANA
Are you insane, talking like this?

ANTIPHOLUS OF SYRACUSE
Not insane, but amazed. I don't know how.

In the original "Shakespearean line, "mated" can mean both "overthrown" and "married."

LUCIANA
Your eyes are playing tricks on you.

ANTIPHOLUS OF SYRACUSE
That's because you are near me, and you're as dazzling as the sun.

LUCIANA
Gaze where you should, and that will clear your sight.

ANTIPHOLUS OF SYRACUSE
As good to wink, sweet love, as look on night.

60 **LUCIANA**
Why call you me "love"? Call my sister so.

ANTIPHOLUS OF SYRACUSE
Thy sister's sister.

LUCIANA
That's my sister.

ANTIPHOLUS OF SYRACUSE
No,
It is thyself, mine own self's better part,
Mine eye's clear eye, my dear heart's dearer heart,
My food, my fortune, and my sweet hope's aim,
65 My sole earth's heaven, and my heaven's claim.

LUCIANA
All this my sister is, or else should be.

ANTIPHOLUS OF SYRACUSE
Call thyself "sister," sweet, for I am thee.
Thee will I love and with thee lead my life;
Thou hast no husband yet, nor I no wife.
70 Give me thy hand.

LUCIANA
O soft, sir! Hold you still.
I'll fetch my sister to get her goodwill.

Exit LUCIANA

Enter DROMIO OF SYRACUSE

ANTIPHOLUS OF SYRACUSE
Why, how now, Dromio. Where runn'st thou so fast?

DROMIO OF SYRACUSE
Do you know me, sir? Am I Dromio? Am I your man? Am
I myself?

LUCIANA

Train your eye on what you should be looking at, and you'll see straight again.

ANTIPHOLUS OF SYRACUSE

Sweet love, I'd rather close my eyes than look at darkness.

LUCIANA

Why are you calling me "love"? Call my sister that.

ANTIPHOLUS OF SYRACUSE

Your sister's sister.

LUCIANA

That's my sister.

ANTIPHOLUS OF SYRACUSE

No, it's you: my better half. My eye's clear vision, my heart's most precious desire. My food, my fortune, my sweetest hope, my heaven on earth, and my entrance to heaven.

LUCIANA

My sister is all those things, or else she should be.

ANTIPHOLUS OF SYRACUSE

Call yourself your own sister, because I want you. I will love you, and with you I'll spend my life. You have no husband yet, and I have no wife. Give me your hand.

LUCIANA

Oh, wait, sir. Stay here. I'll go get my sister and see what she thinks.

LUCIANA *exits.*

DROMIO OF SYRACUSE *enters.*

ANTIPHOLUS OF SYRACUSE

What's going on, Dromio? Where are you running so fast?

DROMIO OF SYRACUSE

Do you know me? Am I Dromio? Am I your servant? Am I myself?

ANTIPHOLUS OF SYRACUSE

75   Thou art Dromio, thou art my man, thou art thyself.

DROMIO OF SYRACUSE

       I am an ass, I am a woman's man, and besides myself.

ANTIPHOLUS OF SYRACUSE

       What woman's man? And how besides thyself?

DROMIO OF SYRACUSE

       Marry, sir, besides myself I am due to a woman, one that
       claims me, one that haunts me, one that will have me.

ANTIPHOLUS OF SYRACUSE

80   What claim lays she to thee?

DROMIO OF SYRACUSE

       Marry, sir, such claim as you would lay to your horse; and
       she would have me as a beast; not that I being a beast she
       would have me, but that she, being a very beastly creature,
       lays claim to me.

ANTIPHOLUS OF SYRACUSE

85   What is she?

DROMIO OF SYRACUSE

       A very reverent body, ay, such a one as a man may not speak
       of without he say "sir-reverence." I have but lean luck in the
       match, and yet is she a wondrous fat marriage.

ANTIPHOLUS OF SYRACUSE

       How dost thou mean a "fat marriage"?

DROMIO OF SYRACUSE

90   Marry, sir, she's the kitchen wench, and all grease, and I
       know not what use to put her to but to make a lamp of her
       and run from her by her own light. I warrant her rags and

ANTIPHOLUS OF SYRACUSE

You are Dromio, you are my servant, and you are yourself.

DROMIO OF SYRACUSE

I'm an ass, I'm a woman's servant, and I'm beside myself.

ANTIPHOLUS OF SYRACUSE

What woman's servant? What do you mean, beside yourself?

DROMIO OF SYRACUSE

I'll tell you. Besides belonging to myself, I belong to a woman. A woman who says she owns me, who won't leave me alone, and who wants me.

ANTIPHOLUS OF SYRACUSE

How does she claim to own you?

DROMIO OF SYRACUSE

The same way a person would claim to own his horse. And she wants me as a beast. I don't mean that she wants me because *I'm* a beast, but that she, who is a beast, says I belong to her.

ANTIPHOLUS OF SYRACUSE

What's she like?

DROMIO OF SYRACUSE

She has a very significant body. You couldn't even talk about it without saying, "I beg your pardon." My luck would be running thin if I ended up with her, although she'd make it a fat marriage.

i.e., you'd have to say "I beg your pardon" when talking about her body because you'd have to use obscene language to discuss it.

ANTIPHOLUS OF SYRACUSE

What do you mean, a fat marriage?

DROMIO OF SYRACUSE

Sir, she works in the kitchen, so she's oily. The only thing I could do with her is to use all that oil as fuel in a lamp and then use that light to run away by. Her

the tallow in them will burn a Poland winter. If she lives till
doomsday, she'll burn a week longer than the whole world.

ANTIPHOLUS OF SYRACUSE
95   What complexion is she of?

DROMIO OF SYRACUSE
Swart like my shoe, but her face nothing like so clean kept.
For why? She sweats. A man may go overshoes in the grime
of it.

ANTIPHOLUS OF SYRACUSE
That's a fault that water will mend.

DROMIO OF SYRACUSE
100   No, sir, 'tis in grain; Noah's flood could not do it.

ANTIPHOLUS OF SYRACUSE
What's her name?

DROMIO OF SYRACUSE
Nell, sir, but her name and three quarters—that's an ell and
three quarters—will not measure her from hip to hip.

ANTIPHOLUS OF SYRACUSE
Then she bears some breadth?

DROMIO OF SYRACUSE
105   No longer from head to foot than from hip to hip. She is
spherical, like a globe. I could find out countries in her.

ANTIPHOLUS OF SYRACUSE
In what part of her body stands Ireland?

DROMIO OF SYRACUSE
Marry, sir, in her buttocks. I found it out by the bogs.

ANTIPHOLUS OF SYRACUSE
Where Scotland?

clothes are so oily, they'd burn through the longest winter. Even if she lives till the end of the world, she'd keep burning an additional week.

ANTIPHOLUS OF SYRACUSE
What's her skin like?

DROMIO OF SYRACUSE
It's dark, like my shoe. But it's not as clean. You'd be up to your ankles in how filthy it is.

ANTIPHOLUS OF SYRACUSE
Some water will fix that.

DROMIO OF SYRACUSE
No, it's permanent. Noah's flood wouldn't be enough water to clean it.

ANTIPHOLUS OF SYRACUSE
What's her name?

DROMIO OF SYRACUSE
Nell. But an ell and three-quarters wouldn't be long enough to measure her waist.

An "ell" is a unit of measure forty-five inches long.

ANTIPHOLUS OF SYRACUSE
So she's wide?

DROMIO OF SYRACUSE
Her hips are as wide as she is tall. She's round, like a globe. I could use her like a map to find out where countries are.

ANTIPHOLUS OF SYRACUSE
What part of her body is Ireland?

DROMIO OF SYRACUSE
Her bottom. It's near the bogs.

ANTIPHOLUS OF SYRACUSE
Where's Scotland?

A "bog" is a kind of swamp found in Ireland, but it's also a slang term for toilet.

DROMIO OF SYRACUSE
110 I found it by the barrenness; hard in the palm of the hand.

ANTIPHOLUS OF SYRACUSE
Where France?

DROMIO OF SYRACUSE
In her forehead, armed and reverted, making war against her heir.

ANTIPHOLUS OF SYRACUSE
Where England?

DROMIO OF SYRACUSE
115 I looked for the chalky cliffs, but I could find no whiteness in them. But I guess it stood in her chin, by the salt rheum that ran between France and it.

ANTIPHOLUS OF SYRACUSE
Where Spain?

DROMIO OF SYRACUSE
Faith, I saw it not, but I felt it hot in her breath.

ANTIPHOLUS OF SYRACUSE
120 Where America, the Indies?

DROMIO OF SYRACUSE

In the palm of her hand, which is covered in calluses.

Shakespeare's audience would hear "barren ness." A "ness" in Scotland is a wide-open space—Nell's calloused palms remind Dromio of the rough, empty terrain of Scotland.

ANTIPHOLUS OF SYRACUSE

Where's France?

DROMIO OF SYRACUSE

In her forehead, which is enormous because of her receding hairline.

At the time this play was written, there had recently been a rebellion against the heir to France's throne. Since Nell is going bald, Dromio puns that her forehead is like France, rebelling against her hair (or "heir").

ANTIPHOLUS OF SYRACUSE

Where's England?

DROMIO OF SYRACUSE

I thought her teeth might be like the white cliffs, but they're dark and stained. So I guess it's her chin, which is separated from her forehead by all the sweat on her face.

The White Cliffs of Dover are located in Southern England, along the English Channel. The cliffs are covered in lime, which renders them white in color.

ANTIPHOLUS OF SYRACUSE

Where's Spain?

DROMIO OF SYRACUSE

Honestly, I didn't see it, but I felt it in her hot breath.

ANTIPHOLUS OF SYRACUSE

Where's America and the West Indies?

DROMIO OF SYRACUSE
O, sir, upon her nose, all o'er-embellished with rubies,
carbuncles, sapphires, declining their rich aspect to the hot
breath of Spain, who sent whole armadas of caracks to be
ballast at her nose.

ANTIPHOLUS OF SYRACUSE
125 Where stood Belgia, the Netherlands?

DROMIO OF SYRACUSE
O, sir, I did not look so low. To conclude: this drudge or
diviner laid claim to me, call'd me Dromio, swore I was
assured to her, told me what privy marks I had about me, as
the mark of my shoulder, the mole in my neck, the great
130 wart on my left arm, that I, amazed, ran from her as a witch.
And, I think, if my breast had not been made of faith, and
        my heart of steel,
She had transformed me to a curtal dog and made me turn
        i' th' wheel.

ANTIPHOLUS OF SYRACUSE
Go, hie thee presently. Post to the road.
An if the wind blow any way from shore,
135 I will not harbor in this town tonight.
If any bark put forth, come to the mart,
Where I will walk till thou return to me.
If every one knows us, and we know none,
'Tis time, I think, to trudge, pack, and be gone.

DROMIO OF SYRACUSE
140 As from a bear a man would run for life,
So fly I from her that would be my wife.

                         Exit DROMIO OF SYRACUSE

ANTIPHOLUS OF SYRACUSE
There's none but witches do inhabit here,
And therefore 'tis high time that I were hence.
She that doth call me husband, even my soul
145 Doth for a wife abhor. But her fair sister,
Possessed with such a gentle sovereign grace,

DROMIO OF SYRACUSE

In Shakespeare's time, America and the West Indies were known for having exotic jewels.

Oh, sir, on her nose, which is covered with pimples, sores, and red welts. It points straight down at her mouth, which catches everything that drips from it.

ANTIPHOLUS OF SYRACUSE

Where's Belgium and the Netherlands?

DROMIO OF SYRACUSE

The Netherlands were known as the "Low Countries."

Oh, sir, I didn't look down there. In conclusion, this witch said I was hers. She called me Dromio and swore I'd promised to marry her. She knew private things about my body, like the birthmark on my shoulder, the mole on my neck, and the huge wart on my left arm. I was terrified, and I ran away from her as if she were a witch. And I think that if I hadn't been brave and strong, she would have turned me into a dog and made me her slave.

ANTIPHOLUS OF SYRACUSE

Get going—hustle over to the port. If there's enough wind for a ship to sail out tonight, I won't spend tonight in this town. If a ship's leaving, come to the marketplace. I'll wait there for you. If everyone here knows us but we don't know anybody, it's time, I think, for us to pack our bags and take off.

DROMIO OF SYRACUSE

I'll run from this woman who claims to be my wife as fast as I'd run from a bear.

DROMIO OF SYRACUSE exits.

ANTIPHOLUS OF SYRACUSE

Everyone who lives here is a witch. That means it's high time for me to go. That woman who claims I am her husband—I loathe her in my soul. But her gorgeous sister, who's so lovely and gracious, who's so charming and who speaks so well,

Of such enchanting presence and discourse,
Hath almost made me traitor to myself.
But lest myself be guilty to self wrong,
150   I'll stop mine ears against the mermaid's song.

Enter ANGELO *with the chain*

ANGELO
Master Antipholus.

ANTIPHOLUS OF SYRACUSE
                     Ay, that's my name.

ANGELO
I know it well, sir. Lo, here's the chain.
I thought to have ta'en you at the Porpentine;
The chain unfinished made me stay thus long.

ANTIPHOLUS OF SYRACUSE
155   What is your will that I shall do with this?

ANGELO
What please yourself, sir. I have made it for you.

ANTIPHOLUS OF SYRACUSE
Made it for me, sir? I bespoke it not.

ANGELO
Not once, nor twice, but twenty times you have.
Go home with it and please your wife withal,
160   And soon at supper time I'll visit you
And then receive my money for the chain.

ANTIPHOLUS OF SYRACUSE
I pray you, sir, receive the money now,
For fear you ne'er see chain nor money more.

ANGELO
You are a merry man, sir. Fare you well.

Exit ANGELO

ANTIPHOLUS OF SYRACUSE
165   What I should think of this I cannot tell,
But this I think: there's no man is so vain
That would refuse so fair an offered chain.

almost makes me want to stay here against my better judgment. I'd better stop up my ears against this siren's song.

ANGELO *enters, with the necklace.*

ANGELO

Master Antipholus—

ANTIPHOLUS OF SYRACUSE

Yes, that's my name.

ANGELO

I know that, sir. Look, here's the necklace.
I was on my way to take it to you at the Porcupine, but it took a little longer to finish than I thought it would.

ANTIPHOLUS OF SYRACUSE

What do you want me to do with this?

ANGELO

Whatever you want—I made it for you.

ANTIPHOLUS OF SYRACUSE

Made it for me? I didn't order it.

ANGELO

You did—not just once or twice, but twenty times. Take it home and make your wife happy. I'll come over at suppertime and you can pay me for it then.

ANTIPHOLUS OF SYRACUSE

You should take the money now. If you don't, you might never see the money or the necklace ever again.

ANGELO

You're a funny man, sir. Take care.

ANGELO *exits.*

ANTIPHOLUS OF SYRACUSE

I don't know what to think about this. But what I do think is that nobody in his right mind would refuse to accept such a beautiful necklace when somebody offers

I see a man here needs not live by shifts
When in the streets he meets such golden gifts.
I'll to the mart, and there for Dromio stay.
170   If any ship put out, then straight away.

Exit

it. I guess there's no need to be a thief in Ephesus.
People come up to you in the street and hand you gold.
I'll go wait for Dromio at the marketplace. If any ships
are sailing, I'll get right on one.

He exits.

ACT FOUR
SCENE 1

Enter SECOND MERCHANT, ANGELO *and an* OFFICER

SECOND MERCHANT
    You know since Pentecost the sum is due,
    And since I have not much importuned you,
    Nor now I had not, but that I am bound
    To Persia, and want guilders for my voyage.
5   Therefore make present satisfaction,
    Or I'll attach you by this officer.

ANGELO
    Even just the sum that I do owe to you
    Is growing to me by Antipholus.
    And in the instant that I met with you,
10   He had of me a chain. At five o'clock
    I shall receive the money for the same.
    Pleaseth you walk with me down to his house,
    I will discharge my bond and thank you too.

Enter ANTIPHOLUS OF EPHESUS *and* DROMIO OF EPHESUS *from the* COURTESAN'S *house*

COURTESAN'S OFFICER
    That labor may you save. See where he comes.

ANTIPHOLUS OF EPHESUS
15   While I go to the goldsmith's house, go thou
    And buy a rope's end. That will I bestow
    Among my wife and her confederates
    For locking me out of my doors by day.
    But soft. I see the goldsmith. Get thee gone.
20   Buy thou a rope, and bring it home to me.

ACT FOUR
SCENE 1

The SECOND MERCHANT, ANGELO, *and an* OFFICER *enter.*

SECOND MERCHANT

You've owed me this money since the Pentecost holiday. I haven't pressed you for it, and I wouldn't now except that I'm going to Persia and I need money for the trip. So pay me now, or I'll have this officer arrest you.

ANGELO

Antipholus owes me the exact amount that I owe you. Just before I ran into you, I gave him a necklace. At five o'clock he's going to pay me for it. Please, come to his house with me. I'll pay what I owe you then and say thank you as well.

ANTIPHOLUS OF EPHESUS *and* DROMIO OF EPHESUS *enter from the* COURTESAN*'s house.*

OFFICER

He saves you the trouble: look, here he comes.

ANTIPHOLUS OF EPHESUS

(to DROMIO*)* I'm going to the jeweler's house. You go buy a piece of rope—I'll whip my wife and her cohorts for locking me out of my own house. Wait a minute! I see the jeweler. Go, be gone with you. Buy a rope and bring it to me.

DROMIO OF EPHESUS
    I buy a thousand pound a year! I buy a rope!

Exit DROMIO OF EPHESUS

ANTIPHOLUS OF EPHESUS
    (to ANGELO*)* A man is well holp up that trusts to you!
    I promisèd your presence and the chain,
    But neither chain nor goldsmith came to me.
25   Belike you thought our love would last too long
    If it were chained together, and therefore came not.

ANGELO
    Saving your merry humor, here's the note
    How much your chain weighs to the utmost carat,
    The fineness of the gold, and chargeful fashion,
30   Which doth amount to three-odd ducats more
    Than I stand debted to this gentleman.
    I pray you, see him presently discharged,
    For he is bound to sea, and stays but for it.

ANTIPHOLUS OF EPHESUS
    I am not furnished with the present money.
35   Besides, I have some business in the town.
    Good signior, take the stranger to my house,
    And with you take the chain, and bid my wife
    Disburse the sum on the receipt thereof.
    Perchance I will be there as soon as you.

ANGELO
40   Then you will bring the chain to her yourself.

ANTIPHOLUS OF EPHESUS
    No, bear it with you lest I come not time enough.

ANGELO
    Well, sir, I will. Have you the chain about you?

ANTIPHOLUS OF EPHESUS
    An if I have not, sir, I hope you have,
    Or else you may return without your money.

DROMIO OF EPHESUS

> I buy myself a thousand beatings a year if I buy a rope.

There's no consensus about the exact meaning of this obscure line, which is an expression of Dromio's frustration.

> **DROMIO OF EPHESUS** *exits.*

ANTIPHOLUS OF EPHESUS

> *(to* ANGELO*)* Good luck to any man who trusts you. I swore that you would come with the necklace, but neither you nor the necklace showed up. Perhaps you were concerned about being chained to me and so decided not to come.

ANGELO

> All joking aside, here's an invoice spelling out exactly how many carats the necklace weighs as well as the quality of the gold and the workmanship. The total due is about three ducats more than I owe this gentleman. Please, pay him immediately. He's about to leave on a trip and he's waiting for the money.

ANTIPHOLUS OF EPHESUS

> I don't have the cash right now. Besides, I have some business to take care of in town. Good signior, take this stranger to my house. Bring the necklace with you, and tell my wife to pay you the amount due. I might make it back in time to meet you.

ANGELO

> So you'll bring the necklace to her yourself?

ANTIPHOLUS OF EPHESUS

> No. You bring it in case I can't make it.

ANGELO

> All right, sir, I will. Do you have it with you?

ANTIPHOLUS OF EPHESUS

> If I don't, I hope you do. Or else you'll leave without your money.

ANGELO

45   Nay, come, I pray you, sir, give me the chain.
          Both wind and tide stays for this gentleman,
          And I, to blame, have held him here too long.

ANTIPHOLUS OF EPHESUS

          Good Lord! You use this dalliance to excuse
          Your breach of promise to the Porpentine.
50   I should have chid you for not bringing it,
          But, like a shrew, you first begin to brawl.

SECOND MERCHANT

          The hour steals on. I pray you, sir, dispatch.

ANGELO

          You hear how he importunes me. The chain!

ANTIPHOLUS OF EPHESUS

          Why, give it to my wife, and fetch your money.

ANGELO

55   Come, come. You know I gave it you even now.
          Either send the chain, or send me by some token.

ANTIPHOLUS OF EPHESUS

          Fie, now you run this humor out of breath.
          Come, where's the chain? I pray you, let me see it.

SECOND MERCHANT

          My business cannot brook this dalliance.
60   (to ANTIPHOLUS) Good sir, say whe'er you'll answer me or no.
          If not, I'll leave him to the Officer.

ANTIPHOLUS OF EPHESUS

          I answer you? What should I answer you?

ANGELO

          The money that you owe me for the chain.

ANTIPHOLUS OF EPHESUS

          I owe you none till I receive the chain.

ANGELO

65   You know I gave it you half an hour since.

ANGELO

> Listen, please, give me the necklace. This gentleman's ready to go. The wind is right and it's high tide, and I've delayed him a long time already.

ANTIPHOLUS OF EPHESUS

> Good Lord! You're using this as an excuse for not showing up at the Porcupine like you promised. I should have reprimanded you then for not bringing it, but you started fighting with me first.

SECOND MERCHANT

> It's getting late. Please, sir, hurry up.

ANGELO

> Antipholus, you hear how the man pleads with me. Give me the necklace!

ANTIPHOLUS OF EPHESUS

> Give it to my wife, and get your money.

ANGELO

> Come, come. You know I gave it to you just now. Send the necklace to her, or send me with a token that will authorize her to pay me.

ANTIPHOLUS OF EPHESUS

> Damn it, this isn't funny. Where's the necklace? Let me see it.

SECOND MERCHANT

> My business cannot wait for this delay. *(to* ANTIPHO-LUS*)* Good sir, tell me if you're going to pay me. If not, I'll turn this man over to the officer.

ANTIPHOLUS OF EPHESUS

> Pay you? What should I pay you?

ANGELO

> The money you owe me for the necklace.

ANTIPHOLUS OF EPHESUS

> I owe you nothing until I receive the necklace.

ANGELO

> You know that I gave it to you a half hour ago.

ANTIPHOLUS OF EPHESUS
> You gave me none. You wrong me much to say so.

ANGELO
> You wrong me more, sir, in denying it.
> Consider how it stands upon my credit.

SECOND MERCHANT
> Well, officer, arrest him at my suit.

OFFICER
70
> I do, *(to* ANGELO*)* and charge you in the Duke's name to
>> obey me.

ANGELO
> This touches me in reputation.
> Either consent to pay this sum for me,
> Or I attach you by this officer.

ANTIPHOLUS OF EPHESUS
> Consent to pay thee that I never had?—
75
> Arrest me, foolish fellow, if thou dar'st.

ANGELO
> Here is thy fee. Arrest him, officer.
> I would not spare my brother in this case
> If he should scorn me so apparently.

OFFICER
> I do arrest you, sir. You hear the suit.

ANTIPHOLUS OF EPHESUS
80
> I do obey thee till I give thee bail.
> But, sirrah, you shall buy this sport as dear
> As all the metal in your shop will answer.

ANGELO
> Sir, sir, I will have law in Ephesus,
> To your notorious shame, I doubt it not.

Enter DROMIO OF SYRACUSE

ANTIPHOLUS OF EPHESUS

> You gave me nothing, and you wrong me by saying you did.

ANGELO

> You wrong me even more, sir, by denying it. Consider how poorly this reflects on me.

SECOND MERCHANT

> Well, officer, I charge you to arrest him.

OFFICER

> I will. (*to* ANGELO) And I order you to obey me, in the name of the duke.

ANGELO

> This harms my reputation. Either pay this sum, Antipholus, or I'll have this officer arrest you.

ANTIPHOLUS OF EPHESUS

> Pay for something I never got? Go ahead, you fool. Arrest me if you dare.

ANGELO

> Officer, here's your fee—arrest him. I would have my own brother arrested if he treated me so terribly.

OFFICER

> You're under arrest, sir. You hear the charges.

ANTIPHOLUS OF EPHESUS

> I'll obey you until I can make bail. But Angelo, you'll pay for this, even if it costs all the precious metals in your jewelry shop.

ANGELO

> Sir, the laws of Ephesus will be on my side, and you'll be embarrassed. I'm certain of it.

DROMIO OF SYRACUSE enters.

DROMIO OF SYRACUSE

85   Master, there is a bark of Epidamnum
        That stays but till her owner comes aboard,
        And then, sir, she bears away. Our fraughtage, sir,
        I have conveyed aboard, and I have bought
        The oil, the balsamum and aqua vitae.
90   The ship is in her trim; the merry wind
        Blows fair from land. They stay for naught at all
        But for their owner, master, and yourself.

ANTIPHOLUS OF EPHESUS

        How now? A madman? Why, thou peevish sheep,
        What ship of Epidamnum stays for me?

DROMIO OF SYRACUSE

95   A ship you sent me to, to hire waftage.

ANTIPHOLUS OF EPHESUS

        Thou drunken slave, I sent thee for a rope
        And told thee to what purpose and what end.

DROMIO OF SYRACUSE

        You sent me for a rope's end as soon.
        You sent me to the bay, sir, for a bark.

ANTIPHOLUS OF EPHESUS

100   I will debate this matter at more leisure
        And teach your ears to list me with more heed.
        To Adriana, villain, hie thee straight.
        Give her this key, and tell her in the desk
        That's cover'd o'er with Turkish tapestry
105   There is a purse of ducats. Let her send it.
        Tell her I am arrested in the street,
        And that shall bail me. Hie thee, slave. Begone.—
        On, officer, to prison till it come.

        Exeunt SECOND MERCHANT, ANGELO, OFFICER, *and* ANTIPHOLUS
                                                        OF EPHESUS

DROMIO OF SYRACUSE

> Master, there's a ship from Epidamnum that's going to set sail as soon as its owner gets on board. I've left our luggage on the ship, and I bought the oil, balm, and liquor you wanted. The ship is ready, the wind is up, and the sailors are only waiting for their owner and for you.

ANTIPHOLUS OF EPHESUS

> What are you, a madman? You annoying idiot, what Epidamnum ship is waiting for me?

DROMIO OF SYRACUSE

> A ship you sent me to find, to book passage out of here.

ANTIPHOLUS OF EPHESUS

> You drunken slave, I sent you for a rope, and I told you what to do with it.

DROMIO OF SYRACUSE

> Yeah, right—you sent me to get whipped. You sent me to the port to find a ship.

ANTIPHOLUS OF EPHESUS

> I'll debate this with you later, and then I'll teach you to listen more carefully. Go to Adriana, you scoundrel, and quickly. Give her this key, and tell her that there's money in the desk that's covered with a Turkish tapestry. Have her send it to me. Tell her that I've been arrested and the money will be my bail. Hurry, you slave! Go! Officer, take me to prison until the money comes.

SECOND MERCHANT, ANGELO, OFFICER, *and* **ANTIPHOLUS OF EPHESUS** *exit.*

DROMIO OF SYRACUSE
To Adriana. That is where we dined,
Where Dowsabel did claim me for her husband.
She is too big, I hope, for me to compass.
Thither I must, although against my will,
For servants must their masters' minds fulfill.

Exit

DROMIO OF SYRACUSE

To Adriana? That's where we had lunch. Where that "sweetheart" said I was her husband! She's too much for me to handle. But I must go there, against my will: servants must fulfill their masters' wishes.

He exits.

ACT 4, SCENE 2

Enter ADRIANA *and* LUCIANA

ADRIANA
Ah, Luciana, did he tempt thee so?
Mightst thou perceive austerely in his eye
That he did plead in earnest, yea or no?
Looked he or red or pale, or sad or merrily?

5   What observation mad'st thou in this case
Of his heart's meteors tilting in his face?

LUCIANA
First he denied you had in him no right.

ADRIANA
He meant he did me none; the more my spite.

LUCIANA
Then swore he that he was a stranger here.

ADRIANA
10   And true he swore, though yet forsworn he were.

LUCIANA
Then pleaded I for you.

ADRIANA
                                And what said he?

LUCIANA
That love I begged for you he begged of me.

ADRIANA
With what persuasion did he tempt thy love?

LUCIANA
With words that in an honest suit might move.
15   First he did praise my beauty, then my speech.

ADRIANA
Did'st speak him fair?

ACT 4, SCENE 2

ADRIANA *and* LUCIANA *enter.*

ADRIANA

Oh, Luciana, did he tempt you like that? Could you tell from his face if he was serious? Yes or no? Did he look flushed or pale? Sad or happy? Could you tell from his looks what he was feeling in his heart?

LUCIANA

First, he said you had no right to him.

ADRIANA

He meant he did nothing right for me—which is true, unfortunately.

LUCIANA

Then he swore he was a stranger here.

ADRIANA

And that's true—he *is* being strange. And yet he lies as well, for he's no stranger.

LUCIANA

Then I pleaded for you.

ADRIANA

And what did he say?

LUCIANA

That he felt for me the love that I begged him to feel for you.

ADRIANA

How did he try to persuade you to love him?

LUCIANA

With words that—if they were spoken honestly—might have moved me. First, he praised my beauty, then my eloquence.

ADRIANA

Did you praise him as well?

LUCIANA
                    Have patience, I beseech.

ADRIANA
          I cannot, nor I will not hold me still;
          My tongue, though not my heart, shall have his will.
          He is deformèd, crooked, old, and sere,
20   Ill-faced, worse-bodied, shapeless everywhere,
          Vicious, ungentle, foolish, blunt, unkind,
          Stigmatical in making, worse in mind.

LUCIANA
          Who would be jealous, then, of such a one?
          No evil lost is wailed when it is gone.

ADRIANA
25   Ah, but I think him better than I say,
          And yet would herein others' eyes were worse.
          Far from her nest the lapwing cries away.
          My heart prays for him, though my tongue do curse.

          Enter DROMIO OF SYRACUSE, *running*

DROMIO OF SYRACUSE
          Here, go—the desk, the purse! Sweet, now make haste.

LUCIANA
30   How hast thou lost thy breath?

DROMIO OF SYRACUSE
                              By running fast.

ADRIANA
          Where is thy master, Dromio? Is he well?

DROMIO OF SYRACUSE
          No, he's in Tartar limbo, worse than hell.
          A devil in an everlasting garment hath him,
          One whose hard heart is buttoned up with steel;
35   A fiend, a fury, pitiless and rough;
          A wolf, nay, worse, a fellow all in buff;
          A back-friend, a shoulder clapper, one that countermands

LUCIANA

Have some patience, please.

ADRIANA

I cannot and I will not keep quiet. My voice will have its way, even if my heart can't. He is misshapen, crooked, old, and withered. His face is ugly, and his body is even worse—all shapeless, everywhere. He is vicious, mean, foolish, blunt, unkind. His body is deformed, and his mind is worse.

LUCIANA

Then why be jealous of a person like that? When an evil thing has been lost, no one cries.

ADRIANA

Oh, but I think of him more highly than I say I do— and I wish he looked worse in other women's eyes. I'm like a lapwing, creating a diversion in order to distract predators from my nest. My heart adores him, even though my tongue curses him.

DROMIO OF SYRACUSE *enters, running.*

DROMIO OF SYRACUSE

Here! Go! The desk! Money! Come on, now! Hurry!

LUCIANA

How did you lose your breath?

DROMIO OF SYRACUSE

By running fast.

ADRIANA

Where's your master, Dromio? Is he all right?

DROMIO OF SYRACUSE

No, he's in a place worse than hell. A devil in a tough uniform has him—a man whose heart is as hard as steel. A fiend and a goblin, pitiless and rough. A wolf—no, even worse—a man all in tough leather. A backbiting friend, one who grabs people, who patrols the streets and passageways. A hunting dog that runs

The passages of alleys, creeks, and narrow lands;
A hound that runs counter and yet draws dryfoot well,
40   One that before the judgment carries poor souls to hell.

ADRIANA
Why, man, what is the matter?

DROMIO OF SYRACUSE
I do not know the matter. He is 'rested on the case.

ADRIANA
What, is he arrested? Tell me at whose suit.

DROMIO OF SYRACUSE
I know not at whose suit he is arrested well,
45   But he's in a suit of buff which 'rested him; that can I tell.
Will you send him, mistress, redemption—the money in
     his desk?

ADRIANA
Go fetch it, sister.

Exit LUCIANA

This I wonder at,
That he, unknown to me, should be in debt.
Tell me, was he arrested on a band?

DROMIO OF SYRACUSE
50   Not on a band, but on a stronger thing:
A chain, a chain. Do you not hear it ring?

ADRIANA
What, the chain?

DROMIO OF SYRACUSE
No, no, the bell. 'Tis time that I were gone.
It was two ere I left him, and now the clock strikes one.

ADRIANA
The hours come back. That did I never hear.

DROMIO OF SYRACUSE
55   O yes, if any hour meet a sergeant, he turns back for
     very fear.

in the opposite direction of its prey, yet can follow the scent of the hunt. A man who puts people away before the verdict is announced.

ADRIANA

Speak, man, what's the matter?

DROMIO OF SYRACUSE

I don't know what the matter is, but he's been arrested for it.

ADRIANA

What? He's been arrested? Tell me, who had him arrested?

DROMIO OF SYRACUSE

I don't know who had him arrested, but the man that arrested him was in a suit of leather. Mistress, will you send him bail? The money in the desk?

ADRIANA

Get it, sister.

LUCIANA *exits.*

I don't understand it. How could he be in debt without me knowing it? Tell me, was he arrested because of a band?

A "band" is a bond or debt. Dromio hears another meaning: a band of fabric.

DROMIO OF SYRACUSE

Not for a band, but for something stronger: a necklace, a necklace! Don't you hear it ring?

ADRIANA

What, the necklace?

DROMIO OF SYRACUSE

No, no, the bell. It's time for me to go. It was two o'clock when I left him, and now it's one.

ADRIANA

Time's running backward? I've never heard of that.

DROMIO OF SYRACUSE

Oh, sure. When an hour meets a cop, it turns and runs in fear.

In Shakespeare's time, "hour" could sound like "ower" (someone who owes money) or even "whore," both of whom would run from policemen.

ADRIANA

As if time were in debt. How fondly dost thou reason!

DROMIO OF SYRACUSE

Time is a very bankrout and owes more than he's worth to
season.
Nay, he's a thief too. Have you not heard men say
That time comes stealing on by night and day?
If he be in debt and theft, and a sergeant in the way,
Hath he not reason to turn back an hour in a day?

Re-enter LUCIANA *with a purse*

ADRIANA

Go, Dromio. There's the money. Bear it straight,
And bring thy master home immediately.
Come, sister, I am pressed down with conceit:
Conceit, my comfort and my injury.

Exeunt

ADRIANA

Time's not the one in debt. Your logic is so foolish.

DROMIO OF SYRACUSE

Time is always bankrupt: it owes more than it can ever pay back in a season. And Time's a thief, too—don't you know the old saying, "Time steals along"? So if Time is in debt and also a thief, and a cop comes, don't you think Time would turn back an hour?

LUCIANA *returns with a purse full of money.*

ADRIANA

Here's the money, Dromio. Take it to your master and bring him home immediately. Come, sister, my imagination is too much for me: it both comforts me and depresses me.

They exit.

ACT 4, SCENE 3

Enter ANTIPHOLUS OF SYRACUSE

ANTIPHOLUS OF SYRACUSE
There's not a man I meet but doth salute me
As if I were their well-acquainted friend,
And every one doth call me by my name.
Some tender money to me; some invite me;
5   Some other give me thanks for kindnesses;
Some offer me commodities to buy.
Even now a tailor called me in his shop
And showed me silks that he had bought for me,
And therewithal took measure of my body.
10   Sure, these are but imaginary wiles,
And Lapland sorcerers inhabit here.

Enter DROMIO OF SYRACUSE

DROMIO OF SYRACUSE
Master, here's the gold you sent me for. What, have you got
the picture of old Adam new-appareled?

ANTIPHOLUS OF SYRACUSE
What gold is this? What Adam dost thou mean?

DROMIO OF SYRACUSE
15   Not that Adam that kept the Paradise, but that Adam that
keeps the prison; he that goes in the calf's skin that was
killed for the Prodigal; he that came behind you, sir, like an
evil angel, and bid you forsake your liberty.

ANTIPHOLUS OF SYRACUSE
I understand thee not.

ACT 4, SCENE 3

ANTIPHOLUS OF SYRACUSE *enters.*

ANTIPHOLUS OF SYRACUSE
Every person I meet greets me like an old friend, and every one of them knows my name. Some of them give me money, some invite me places, some thank me for the kind things I've done for them, some try to sell me things. Just now a tailor showed me fabrics he bought especially for me and then started to take my measurements. These are tricks of the imagination, and this place is filled with magicians.

DROMIO OF SYRACUSE *enters.*

DROMIO OF SYRACUSE
Here's the money you wanted, master. Hey, have you gotten rid of that Adam?

Dromio calls the officer "Adam" because, after Adam and Eve were expelled from Eden, Adam wore clothing made of skins, llike the officer's leather uniform.

ANTIPHOLUS OF SYRACUSE
What gold is this? Who's this Adam you speak of?

DROMIO OF SYRACUSE
Not the Adam from the garden of Eden, but the Adam from the jailhouse. The one that wears leather clothes. The one that grabbed you and arrested you.

ANTIPHOLUS OF SYRACUSE
I don't know what you're talking about.

DROMIO OF SYRACUSE

20 No? Why, 'tis a plain case: he that went, like a bass viol in
a case of leather; the man, sir, that, when gentlemen are
tired, gives them a sob and 'rests them; he, sir, that takes
pity on decayed men and gives them suits of durance; he
that sets up his rest to do more exploits with his mace than
25 a morris-pike.

ANTIPHOLUS OF SYRACUSE

What, thou meanest an officer?

DROMIO OF SYRACUSE

Ay, sir, the sergeant of the band; he that brings any man to
answer it that breaks his band; one that thinks a man always
going to bed and says "God give you good rest."

ANTIPHOLUS OF SYRACUSE

30 Well, sir, there rest in your foolery. Is there any ships put
forth tonight? May we be gone?

DROMIO OF SYRACUSE

Why, sir, I brought you word an hour since that the bark
Expedition put forth tonight, and then were you hindered
by the sergeant to tarry for the hoy *Delay.* Here are the
35 angels that you sent for to deliver you.

ANTIPHOLUS OF SYRACUSE

The fellow is distract, and so am I,
And here we wander in illusions.
Some blessed power deliver us from hence!

Enter a COURTESAN

COURTESAN

Well met, well met, Master Antipholus.
40 I see, sir, you have found the goldsmith now.
Is that the chain you promised me today?

ANTIPHOLUS OF SYRACUSE

Satan, avoid! I charge thee, tempt me not.

DROMIO OF SYRACUSE

Master, is this Mistress Satan?

DROMIO OF SYRACUSE

No? It's plain enough. The Adam who looks like a cello, in a big leather case. The one who gives tired people "arrest." The one who gives ruined men new suits—law suits. The one who's determined to do more damage with his nightstick than a soldier does with his pike.

ANTIPHOLUS OF SYRACUSE

You mean an officer?

DROMIO OF SYRACUSE

Yes, the leader of the team; the one that gets you if you can't pay a debt; the one who assumes people are always going to bed and says to them, "Have arrest."

ANTIPHOLUS OF SYRACUSE

Well, sir, stop your joking there. Are any ships leaving tonight? Can we go?

DROMIO OF SYRACUSE

Why, sir, I told you an hour ago that the good ship *Expedition* was leaving tonight, but then the officer got you, and you decided to wait for the little rowboat *Delay.* Here's the bail money you sent me to get.

ANTIPHOLUS OF SYRACUSE

This fellow's gone mad, and so have I. We're in some kind of dream world. Please, somebody, get us out of here!

A COURTESAN *enters.*

COURTESAN

Good to see you, Master Antipholus. I see you've met with the jeweler. Is that chain you're wearing the one you promised to give to me?

ANTIPHOLUS OF SYRACUSE

Get away from me, Satan! Don't try to tempt me!

DROMIO OF SYRACUSE

Master, is this Satan's mistress?

ANTIPHOLUS OF SYRACUSE
It is the devil.

DROMIO OF SYRACUSE

45   Nay, she is worse; she is the devil's dam, and here she comes
in the habit of a light wench. And thereof comes that the
wenches say "God damn me"; that's as much to say "God
make me a light wench." It is written they appear to men
like angels of light. Light is an effect of fire, and fire will

50   burn: ergo, light wenches will burn. Come not near her.

COURTESAN
Your man and you are marvelous merry, sir.
Will you go with me? We'll mend our dinner here.

DROMIO OF SYRACUSE
Master, if you do, expect spoon meat; or bespeak a long
spoon.

ANTIPHOLUS OF SYRACUSE

55   Why, Dromio?

DROMIO OF SYRACUSE
Marry, he must have a long spoon that must eat with the
devil.

ANTIPHOLUS OF SYRACUSE
(*to* COURTESAN) Avoid then, fiend! What tell'st thou me of
supping?
Thou art, as you are all, a sorceress.

60   I conjure thee to leave me and be gone.

COURTESAN
Give me the ring of mine you had at dinner
Or, for my diamond, the chain you promised,
And I'll be gone, sir, and not trouble you.

ANTIPHOLUS OF SYRACUSE

She's the devil.

DROMIO OF SYRACUSE

No, she's worse: she's the devil's mother, and she comes to us disguised as an easy wench. And that's why some women say, "God damn me," which is the same thing as saying, "God make me an easy wench." The Bible says the devil looks like an angel of light. But fire also gives off light, and fire will burn you. In other words, easy wenches will burn you. Keep away from this one.

COURTESAN

You and your servant are very funny, sir. Will you come with me? Can we finish our lunch?

DROMIO OF SYRACUSE

Master, if you eat with her, bring really long silverware.

ANTIPHOLUS OF SYRACUSE

Why, Dromio?

DROMIO OF SYRACUSE

Because of the old saying: "He who eats with the devil needs a very long spoon." You need to keep far away from them.

ANTIPHOLUS OF SYRACUSE

(to COURTESAN) Get away, you demon! You talk about eating? You're a sorceress, like everyone else here. I'll conjure you, like a spell: get away from me.

COURTESAN

Give me back the ring I gave you at lunch, or give me the necklace you promised in exchange. Then I'll be gone, sir, and stop troubling you.

DROMIO OF SYRACUSE

Some devils ask but the parings of one's nail, a rush, a hair,
65   a drop of blood, a pin, a nut, a cherrystone; but she, more
covetous, would have a chain. Master, be wise. An if you
give it her, the devil will shake her chain and fright us with it.

COURTESAN

I pray you, sir, my ring or else the chain.
I hope you do not mean to cheat me so.

ANTIPHOLUS OF SYRACUSE

70   Avaunt, thou witch!—Come, Dromio, let us go.

DROMIO OF SYRACUSE

"Fly pride," says the peacock. Mistress, that you know.

Exeunt **ANTIPHOLUS OF SYRACUSE**
and **DROMIO OF SYRACUSE**

COURTESAN

Now, out of doubt Antipholus is mad;
Else would he never so demean himself.
75   A ring he hath of mine worth forty ducats,
And for the same he promised me a chain.
Both one and other he denies me now.
The reason that I gather he is mad,
Besides this present instance of his rage,
80   Is a mad tale he told today at dinner
Of his own doors being shut against his entrance.
Belike his wife, acquainted with his fits,
On purpose shut the doors against his way.
My way is now to hie home to his house
85   And tell his wife that, being lunatic,
He rushed into my house and took perforce
My ring away. This course I fittest choose,
For forty ducats is too much to lose.

Exit

DROMIO OF SYRACUSE

Some devils ask for nothing more than nail clippings, a hair, a drop of blood, a pin, a nut, or a cherry pit. But this one's greedy: she wants a necklace. Be wise, master. If you give it to her, she'll shake the chain and frighten us, like the angel in the Bible.

COURTESAN

Now listen, either give me my ring or give me the necklace. I hope you're not trying to cheat me.

ANTIPHOLUS OF SYRACUSE

Be gone, witch! Come, Dromio, let's go.

DROMIO OF SYRACUSE

Accusing us of cheating is like the proud peacock accusing someone else of pride. Mistress, you know about that.

ANTIPHOLUS OF SYRACUSE and DROMIO OF SYRACUSE exit.

COURTESAN

Antipholus has gone insane, no question about it. If not, he'd never behave like this. He has a ring of mine, worth forty ducats, and he promised to give me a necklace in exchange for it. Now he won't give me either. The reason I think he's insane, besides the way he just acted, is that he told a senseless story over lunch about being locked out of his own house. His wife probably did it on purpose because she knows what kind of fits he's having. I must go to his house and tell his wife that he came bursting into my place like a lunatic and stole my ring. It's my best option: I can't afford to lose forty ducats.

She exits.

ACT 4, SCENE 4

Enter ANTIPHOLUS OF EPHESUS *and the* OFFICER

ANTIPHOLUS OF EPHESUS
    Fear me not, man. I will not break away:
    I'll give thee, ere I leave thee, so much money,
    To warrant thee, as I am 'rested for.
5   My wife is in a wayward mood today
    And will not lightly trust the messenger
    That I should be attached in Ephesus.
    I tell you, 'twill sound harshly in her ears.

Enter DROMIO OF EPHESUS *with a rope's end*

    Here comes my man. I think he brings the money.
    How now, sir? Have you that I sent you for?

10 DROMIO OF EPHESUS
    Here's that, I warrant you, will pay them all.

ANTIPHOLUS OF EPHESUS
    But where's the money?

DROMIO OF EPHESUS
    Why, sir, I gave the money for the rope.

ANTIPHOLUS OF EPHESUS
    Five hundred ducats, villain, for a rope?

DROMIO OF EPHESUS
    I'll serve you, sir, five hundred at the rate.

15 ANTIPHOLUS OF EPHESUS
    To what end did I bid thee hie thee home?

DROMIO OF EPHESUS
    To a rope's end, sir, and to that end am I returned.

ANTIPHOLUS OF EPHESUS
    And to that end, sir, I will welcome you. *(beats* DROMIO
        OF EPHESUS*)*

ACT 4, SCENE 4

ANTIPHOLUS OF EPHESUS *enters with the* OFFICER.

ANTIPHOLUS OF EPHESUS

Don't worry, man, I won't try to escape. When it's time for me to be freed, I'll pay you the fee you're entitled to for arresting me. My wife's in a perverse mood today. She'll be suspicious when the messenger tells her that I was arrested. I tell you, this will make her angry when she hears about it.

DROMIO OF EPHESUS *enters, holding a length of rope.*

Here's my servant. I think he's got the money. Hello there, sir! Do you have what I told you to get?

DROMIO OF EPHESUS

Yes. And this rope will take care of everybody, I guarantee it.

ANTIPHOLUS OF EPHESUS

But where's the money?

DROMIO OF EPHESUS

Why, sir, I spent it on this rope.

ANTIPHOLUS OF EPHESUS

You idiot! Five hundred ducats for a rope?

DROMIO OF EPHESUS

I can get you five hundred ropes for that price.

ANTIPHOLUS OF EPHESUS

Why did I just send you home?

DROMIO OF EPHESUS

To get a piece of rope. And here I am, with that piece.

ANTIPHOLUS OF EPHESUS

And I'll use that piece of rope to welcome you with.
(beats DROMIO OF EPHESUS*)*

OFFICER
Good sir, be patient.

DROMIO OF EPHESUS
Nay, 'tis for me to be patient. I am in adversity.

OFFICER
20   Good now, hold thy tongue.

DROMIO OF EPHESUS
Nay, rather persuade him to hold his hands.

ANTIPHOLUS OF EPHESUS
Thou whoreson, senseless villain.

DROMIO OF EPHESUS
I would I were senseless, sir, that I might not feel your
blows.

ANTIPHOLUS OF EPHESUS
Thou art sensible in nothing but blows, and so is an ass.

DROMIO OF EPHESUS
25   I am an ass, indeed; you may prove it by my long ears.—I
have served him from the hour of my nativity to this
instant, and have nothing at his hands for my service but
blows. When I am cold, he heats me with beating; when I
am warm, he cools me with beating. I am waked with it
30   when I sleep, raised with it when I sit, driven out of doors
with it when I go from home, welcomed home with it when
I return. Nay, I bear it on my shoulders as a beggar wont her
brat, and I think when he hath lamed me, I shall beg with it
from door to door.

ANTIPHOLUS OF EPHESUS
35   Come, go along. My wife is coming yonder.

Enter ADRIANA, LUCIANA, *the* COURTESAN *and a
schoolmaster called* PINCH

OFFICER

Good sir, calm down.

DROMIO OF EPHESUS

You should tell me to calm down—I'm the one who's suffering here.

OFFICER

Hold your tongue.

DROMIO OF EPHESUS

No, you should tell him to hold his hands!

ANTIPHOLUS OF EPHESUS

You son of a bitch, senseless villain!

DROMIO OF EPHESUS

I wish I were senseless, sir, so that I wouldn't feel your punches!

ANTIPHOLUS OF EPHESUS

The only thing you can sense are punches—just like an ass.

DROMIO OF EPHESUS

I am an ass, indeed: you can tell by my long ears. I've served this man from the moment I was born until this very instant, and all I've ever gotten from him are bruises. When I'm cold, his beatings keep me warm. When I'm hot, they keep me cool. He wakes me up by beating me, makes me stand by beating me, sends me out of the house and welcomes me back by beating me. Seriously, I carry beatings around with me like a beggar woman carries her baby. I figure that once he's crippled me, I'll beg by showing off my beatings.

ANTIPHOLUS OF EPHESUS

That's enough. My wife's coming.

ADRIANA, LUCIANA, *the* COURTESAN, *and* PINCH, *a schoolmaster, enter.*

DROMIO OF EPHESUS
> Mistress, *respice finem*, respect your end, or rather, the
> prophecy like the parrot, "Beware the rope's end."

ANTIPHOLUS OF EPHESUS
> Wilt thou still talk? *(beats* DROMIO OF EPHESUS*)*

COURTESAN
> How say you now? Is not your husband mad?

ADRIANA
40 > His incivility confirms no less.—
> Good Doctor Pinch, you are a conjurer;
> Establish him in his true sense again,
> And I will please you what you will demand.

LUCIANA
> Alas, how fiery and how sharp he looks!

COURTESAN
45 > Mark how he trembles in his ecstasy.

PINCH
> Give me your hand, and let me feel your pulse.

ANTIPHOLUS OF EPHESUS
> There is my hand, and let it feel your ear. *(strikes* PINCH*)*

PINCH
> I charge thee, Satan, housed within this man,
> To yield possession to my holy prayers
50 > And to thy state of darkness hie thee straight.
> I conjure thee by all the saints in heaven.

ANTIPHOLUS OF EPHESUS
> Peace, doting wizard, peace. I am not mad.

ADRIANA
> O, that thou wert not, poor distressèd soul!

ANTIPHOLUS OF EPHESUS
> You minion, you, are these your customers?
55 > Did this companion with the saffron face
> Revel and feast it at my house today

DROMIO OF EPHESUS

Mistress, think about your end—beware of your death! Or as the parrot says: "Beware of the *rope's* end," and watch out for a hanging.

ANTIPHOLUS OF EPHESUS

Are you going to keep talking? *(beats* DROMIO OF EPHESUS*)*

COURTESAN

Now what do you think? Your husband's mad, isn't he?

ADRIANA

This terrible behavior proves it. Doctor Pinch, you're an exorcist. If you can bring him back to his senses, I'll pay you whatever you demand.

LUCIANA

Alas, how passionate and angry he looks!

COURTESAN

Look! He's trembling in his fit!

PINCH

Give me your hand. Let me take your pulse.

ANTIPHOLUS OF EPHESUS

Here's my hand. Let it feel your ear. *(he strikes* PINCH*)*

PINCH

Satan! You are living inside this man! I order you to release him through my prayers and to return immediately to the darkness you came from. I demand this in the name of all the saints in heaven.

ANTIPHOLUS OF EPHESUS

Shut up, you doddering old wizard! I'm not possessed!

ADRIANA

Oh, I wish you weren't, you poor, frightened soul.

ANTIPHOLUS OF EPHESUS

Listen, hussy—is this man one of your customers? Did this fool with the yellow face feast and celebrate in my house today while the guilty doors shut in my face and locked me out of my own house?

Whilst upon me the guilty doors were shut
And I denied to enter in my house?

ADRIANA

O husband, God doth know you dined at home,
60 Where would you had remained until this time,
Free from these slanders and this open shame.

ANTIPHOLUS OF EPHESUS

"Dined at home"? Thou villain, what sayest thou?

DROMIO OF EPHESUS

Sir, sooth to say, you did not dine at home.

ANTIPHOLUS OF EPHESUS

Were not my doors locked up and I shut out?

DROMIO OF EPHESUS

65 Perdie, your doors were locked, and you shut out.

ANTIPHOLUS OF EPHESUS

And did not she herself revile me there?

DROMIO OF EPHESUS

Sans fable, she herself reviled you there.

ANTIPHOLUS OF EPHESUS

Did not her kitchen maid rail, taunt, and scorn me?

DROMIO OF EPHESUS

Certes, she did; the kitchen vestal scorned you.

ANTIPHOLUS OF EPHESUS

70 And did not I in rage depart from thence?

DROMIO OF EPHESUS

In verity you did.—My bones bear witness,
That since have felt the vigour of his rage.

ADRIANA

(to PINCH*)* Is't good to soothe him in these contraries?

PINCH

It is no shame. The fellow finds his vein
75 And, yielding to him, humors well his frenzy.

ANTIPHOLUS OF EPHESUS

(to ADRIANA*)* Thou hast suborned the goldsmith to arrest me.

ADRIANA

Oh, husband, God himself knows you ate at home. I wish you had stayed there, avoiding these scandals and this public embarrassment!

ANTIPHOLUS OF EPHESUS

Ate at home? You there, rogue, what do you have to say about that?

DROMIO OF EPHESUS

I swear, sir, you did not eat at home.

ANTIPHOLUS OF EPHESUS

My doors were locked and I was shut out, right?

DROMIO OF EPHESUS

By God, your doors were locked and you were shut out.

ANTIPHOLUS OF EPHESUS

And she screamed at me, right?

DROMIO OF EPHESUS

No lie—she screamed at you.

ANTIPHOLUS OF EPHESUS

And her cook yelled, mocked, and teased me, right?

DROMIO OF EPHESUS

She sure did. The kitchen girl mocked you.

ANTIPHOLUS OF EPHESUS

And I departed in a rage, right?

DROMIO OF EPHESUS

You truly did. My body can prove it because it felt the power of your anger.

ADRIANA

(to PINCH) Should I try to soothe him by pretending to agree with his lies?

PINCH

Good idea. His servant here has figured out that agreeing is a good way to cope with his anger.

ANTIPHOLUS OF EPHESUS

(to ADRIANA) You convinced the jeweler to arrest me.

ADRIANA
　　　　Alas, I sent you money to redeem you
　　　　By Dromio here, who came in haste for it.

DROMIO OF EPHESUS
　　　　Money by me! heart and goodwill you might,
80　　　But surely, master, not a rag of money.

ANTIPHOLUS OF EPHESUS
　　　　Went'st not thou to her for a purse of ducats?

ADRIANA
　　　　He came to me, and I delivered it.

LUCIANA
　　　　And I am witness with her that she did.

DROMIO OF EPHESUS
　　　　God and the rope-maker bear me witness
85　　　That I was sent for nothing but a rope.

PINCH
　　　　Mistress, both man and master is possessed.
　　　　I know it by their pale and deadly looks.
　　　　They must be bound and laid in some dark room.

ANTIPHOLUS OF EPHESUS
　　　　(to ADRIANA*)* Say wherefore didst thou lock me forth today.
90　　　*(to* DROMIO OF EPHESUS*)* And why dost thou deny the bag of
　　　　　　　gold?

ADRIANA
　　　　I did not, gentle husband, lock thee forth.

DROMIO OF EPHESUS
　　　　And, gentle master, I received no gold.
　　　　But I confess, sir, that we were locked out.

ADRIANA
　　　　Dissembling villain, thou speak'st false in both.

ANTIPHOLUS OF EPHESUS
95　　　Dissembling harlot, thou art false in all,
　　　　And art confederate with a damnèd pack
　　　　To make a loathsome abject scorn of me.

ADRIANA

For goodness sake, I sent money to bail you out. I gave it to Dromio, who rushed in for it.

DROMIO OF EPHESUS

You gave money to me? She might have given me her best wishes, master, but she didn't give me one scrap of money.

ANTIPHOLUS OF EPHESUS

Didn't you go to her for a purse full of ducats?

ADRIANA

He did, and I gave it to him.

LUCIANA

And I saw her do it.

DROMIO OF EPHESUS

I was sent for a rope! God and the rope maker are my witnesses!

PINCH

Mistress, both the man and his master are possessed. I can tell by how pale and deathlike they look. We must tie them up and leave them in some dark room.

ANTIPHOLUS OF EPHESUS

(*to* ADRIANA) Tell me! Why did you lock me out today? (*to* DROMIO OF EPHESUS) And why are you denying that you received the gold?

ADRIANA

My sweet husband, I did not lock you out.

DROMIO OF EPHESUS

And my sweet master, I received no gold. But I agree, sir, that we were locked out.

ADRIANA

You lying villain! Both those statements are false.

ANTIPHOLUS OF EPHESUS

You lying slut, everything you say is false. You're scheming with some damned gang, trying to make a fool of me. With my own bare hands, I'll scratch out your eyes, which want to see me humiliated.

But with these nails I'll pluck out these false eyes
That would behold in me this shameful sport.

Enter three or four, and offer to bind him. He strives.

ADRIANA
100   O bind him, bind him! Let him not come near me.

PINCH
More company! The fiend is strong within him.

LUCIANA
Ay me, poor man, how pale and wan he looks!

ANTIPHOLUS OF EPHESUS
What, will you murder me?—Thou jailer, thou,
I am thy prisoner. Wilt thou suffer them
105   To make a rescue?

OFFICER
                Masters, let him go.
He is my prisoner, and you shall not have him.

PINCH
Go, bind this man, for he is frantic too.

They bind DROMIO OF EPHESUS

ADRIANA
What wilt thou do, thou peevish officer?
Hast thou delight to see a wretched man
110   Do outrage and displeasure to himself?

OFFICER
He is my prisoner. If I let him go,
The debt he owes will be required of me.

ADRIANA
I will discharge thee ere I go from thee.
Bear me forthwith unto his creditor,
115   And, knowing how the debt grows, I will pay it.—
Good Master Doctor, see him safe conveyed
Home to my house. O most unhappy day!

Three or four men enter and try to restrain ANTIPHOLUS
OF EPHESUS. *He struggles with them.*

ADRIANA

Tie him up! Tie him up! Keep him away from me!

PINCH

We need more help! The devil in him is strong!

LUCIANA

Oh, my, poor man! How pale and listless he looks!

ANTIPHOLUS OF EPHESUS

Are you trying to kill me? Jailer, I'm your prisoner.
Are you going to let them break me out of jail?

OFFICER

Gentlemen, let go of him. He's my prisoner and you
can't have him.

PINCH

Tie up the servant, for he is mad as well.

The men tie up DROMIO OF EPHESUS.

ADRIANA

What are you doing, you stupid officer? Do you take
some kind of pleasure in seeing a sick man harm
himself?

OFFICER

He's my prisoner. If I let him go, I'll have to pay his
bail fees myself.

ADRIANA

I'll pay you. Take me to the man my husband is in debt
to. Once I find out what the debt is for, I'll pay it. Doctor Pinch, please have him brought to my house. What
a horrible day!

ANTIPHOLUS OF EPHESUS
O most unhappy strumpet!

DROMIO OF EPHESUS
Master, I am here entered in bond for you.

ANTIPHOLUS OF EPHESUS
120   Out on thee, villain! Wherefore dost thou mad me?

DROMIO OF EPHESUS
Will you be bound for nothing? Be mad, good master.
Cry "The devil!"

LUCIANA
God help poor souls! How idly do they talk!

ADRIANA
Go bear him hence. Sister, go you with me.

Exeunt PINCH *and the men, with* ANTIPHOLUS OF
EPHESUS *and* DROMIO OF EPHESUS

Manent OFFICER, ADRIANA, LUCIANA, COURTESAN

125   Say now whose suit is he arrested at.

OFFICER
One Angelo, a goldsmith. Do you know him?

ADRIANA
I know the man. What is the sum he owes?

OFFICER
Two hundred ducats.

ADRIANA
                        Say, how grows it due?

OFFICER
Due for a chain your husband had of him.

ADRIANA
130   He did bespeak a chain for me but had it not.

ANTIPHOLUS OF EPHESUS

What a horrible slut!

DROMIO OF EPHESUS

Master, I'm all tied up for you.

ANTIPHOLUS OF EPHESUS

Shut up already, you scoundrel! Why are you trying to provoke me?

DROMIO OF EPHESUS

You'd rather be tied up for nothing? Act insane, good master: scream out, "The devil!"

LUCIANA

Oh my God! The poor souls—how strangely they talk!

ADRIANA

Get him out of here. Sister, come with me.

> PINCH *and the men lead* ANTIPHOLUS OF EPHESUS *and* DROMIO OF EPHESUS *offstage.*

> *The* OFFICER, ADRIANA, LUCIANA, *and the* COURTESAN *remain onstage.*

Now tell me. Who had him arrested?

OFFICER

Angelo, the jeweler. Do you know him?

ADRIANA

I know him. How much does my husband owe?

OFFICER

Two hundred ducats.

ADRIANA

For what?

OFFICER

For a necklace your husband had him make.

ADRIANA

He said he was going to buy me a necklace, but I never saw it.

COURTESAN
>Whenas your husband all in rage today
>Came to my house and took away my ring,
>The ring I saw upon his finger now,
>Straight after did I meet him with a chain.

ADRIANA
135
>It may be so, but I did never see it.—
>Come, jailer, bring me where the goldsmith is.
>I long to know the truth hereof at large.

Enter ANTIPHOLUS OF SYRACUSE *with his rapier drawn and*
DROMIO OF SYRACUSE

LUCIANA
>God for Thy mercy, they are loose again!

ADRIANA
>And come with naked swords. Let's call more help
140
>To have them bound again.

OFFICER
>   Away! They'll kill us.

Run all out as fast as may be, frighted.

ANTIPHOLUS OF SYRACUSE
>I see these witches are afraid of swords.

DROMIO OF SYRACUSE
>She that would be your wife now ran from you.

ANTIPHOLUS OF SYRACUSE
>Come to the Centaur. Fetch our stuff from thence.
>I long that we were safe and sound aboard.

DROMIO OF SYRACUSE
145
>Faith, stay here this night. They will surely do us no harm.
>You saw they speak us fair, give us gold. Methinks they are
>such a gentle nation that, but for the mountain of mad flesh

COURTESAN

> Today your husband came to my place, completely furious. He took my ring, which I just saw on his finger, by the way. Right after that, I saw him with a necklace.

ADRIANA

> Maybe so, but I never saw it. Jailer, bring me to the jeweler. I need to hear the truth about all this.

ANTIPHOLUS OF SYRACUSE enters with his sword drawn, followed by DROMIO OF SYRACUSE.

LUCIANA

> God have mercy on us! They broke loose!

ADRIANA

> And they've got their swords unsheathed! Let's call for help and get them tied up again!

OFFICER

> Let's get out of here! They'll kill us!

Frightened, ADRIANA, LUCIANA, the OFFICER, and the COURTESAN run offstage as fast as they can.

ANTIPHOLUS OF SYRACUSE

> It looks like these witches are scared of swords.

DROMIO OF SYRACUSE

> The one who claims to be your wife just ran away from you.

ANTIPHOLUS OF SYRACUSE

> Go to the Centaur and get our stuff. I wish we were safely on board our ship already.

DROMIO OF SYRACUSE

> Look, let's stay here tonight. Nobody will hurt us. You see how kind everyone is to us, how they just hand us gold. I think this country is so kind that if it weren't for

that claims marriage of me, I could find in my heart to stay
here still, and turn witch.

ANTIPHOLUS OF SYRACUSE
150   I will not stay tonight for all the town.
        Therefore away, to get our stuff aboard.

Exeunt

that mountain of insanity that wants to marry me, I could find it in my heart to stay here and become a witch myself.

ANTIPHOLUS OF SYRACUSE

I wouldn't stay here tonight for the entire town. Go and get our stuff onto the ship.

They exit.

ACT FIVE
SCENE 1

Enter SECOND MERCHANT *and* ANGELO *the goldsmith*

ANGELO
I am sorry, sir, that I have hindered you,
But I protest he had the chain of me,
Though most dishonestly he doth deny it.

SECOND MERCHANT
How is the man esteemed here in the city?

ANGELO
5   Of very reverend reputation, sir,
Of credit infinite, highly beloved,
Second to none that lives here in the city.
His word might bear my wealth at any time.

SECOND MERCHANT
Speak softly. Yonder, as I think, he walks.

ANTIPHOLUS OF SYRACUSE *and* DROMIO OF SYRACUSE *again*

ANGELO
10   'Tis so; and that self chain about his neck
Which he forswore most monstrously to have.
Good sir, draw near to me. I'll speak to him.—
Signior Antipholus, I wonder much
That you would put me to this shame and trouble,
15   And not without some scandal to yourself,
With circumstance and oaths so to deny
This chain, which now you wear so openly.
Beside the charge, the shame, imprisonment,
You have done wrong to this my honest friend,
20   Who, but for staying on our controversy,

ACT FIVE
SCENE 1

The SECOND MERCHANT *and* ANGELO *enter.*

ANGELO

I'm sorry that I delayed you, sir. But even though he denies it, I swear he got the necklace from me.

SECOND MERCHANT

What's this man's reputation like here in the city?

ANGELO

People think very highly of him. The merchants give him unlimited credit. He's well beloved, second to none in the city. I'd trust him with everything I own.

SECOND MERCHANT

Speak more quietly: I think he's coming this way.

ANTIPHOLUS OF SYRACUSE *and* DROMIO OF SYRACUSE *enter.*

ANGELO

You're right. And that necklace around his neck is the very one he swore he didn't have! Good sir, stay close to me. I'll speak to him. Signior Antipholus, I can't believe you'd put me to this kind of shame and trouble—not to mention the scandal you've brought on yourself. You swore I never gave you the necklace, but now you're wearing it openly. Not only has your lie cost you money, shame, and imprisonment, but you've also mistreated this honest friend of mine. If it hadn't been for this dispute, he would have already hoisted sail and left for sea. You got that necklace from me: can you deny that?

Had hoisted sail and put to sea today.
This chain you had of me. Can you deny it?

ANTIPHOLUS OF SYRACUSE
I think I had. I never did deny it.

SECOND MERCHANT
Yes, that you did, sir, and forswore it too.

ANTIPHOLUS OF SYRACUSE
25 Who heard me to deny it or forswear it?

SECOND MERCHANT
These ears of mine, thou know'st did hear thee.
Fie on thee, wretch. 'Tis pity that thou liv'st
To walk where any honest men resort.

ANTIPHOLUS OF SYRACUSE
Thou art a villain to impeach me thus.
30 I'll prove mine honor and mine honesty
Against thee presently if thou dar'st stand.

SECOND MERCHANT
I dare, and do defy thee for a villain.

They draw
Enter ADRIANA, LUCIANA, *the* COURTESAN *and others*

ADRIANA
Hold, hurt him not, for God's sake. He is mad.—
Some get within him; take his sword away.
35 Bind Dromio too, and bear them to my house!

DROMIO OF SYRACUSE
Run, master, run. For God's sake, take a house.
This is some priory. In, or we are spoiled.

Exeunt ANTIPHOLUS OF SYRACUSE *and* DROMIO OF
SYRACUSE *to the priory*

Enter the Lady ABBESS

ANTIPHOLUS OF SYRACUSE
I got it from you—I never said I didn't.

SECOND MERCHANT
Yes, you did, sir. In fact, you swore it.

ANTIPHOLUS OF SYRACUSE
Who heard me do that?

SECOND MERCHANT
My own ears heard it, and you know it. To hell with you! It's a shame that you walk the streets with all the honest men.

ANTIPHOLUS OF SYRACUSE
You're a villain to say this about me. I'll prove that I'm an honest man and a man of honor if you dare defend yourself.

SECOND MERCHANT
I do dare, and I say that you are the villain.

They draw their swords. ADRIANA, LUCIANA, *the* COURTESAN, *and others enter.*

ADRIANA

(to SECOND MERCHANT*)* Wait! Don't hurt him, for God's sake! He's crazy! Somebody approach him and take away his sword. Tie up Dromio, too, and take them to my house.

DROMIO OF SYRACUSE
Run, master, run. For God's sake, find a house to duck into. This looks like an abbey. Go in, or we're done for.

ANTIPHOLUS OF SYRACUSE *and* DROMIO OF
SYRACUSE *exit into the abbey.*

The ABBESS *enters.*

ABBESS
Be quiet, people. Wherefore throng you hither?

ADRIANA
To fetch my poor distracted husband hence.
40   Let us come in, that we may bind him fast
And bear him home for his recovery.

ANGELO
I knew he was not in his perfect wits.

SECOND MERCHANT
I am sorry now that I did draw on him.

ABBESS
How long hath this possession held the man?

ADRIANA
45   This week he hath been heavy, sour, sad,
And much different from the man he was.
But till this afternoon his passion
Ne'er brake into extremity of rage.

ABBESS
Hath he not lost much wealth by wrack of sea?
50   Buried some dear friend? Hath not else his eye
Stray'd his affection in unlawful love,
A sin prevailing much in youthful men
Who give their eyes the liberty of gazing?
Which of these sorrows is he subject to?

ADRIANA
55   To none of these, except it be the last,
Namely, some love that drew him oft from home.

ABBESS
You should for that have reprehended him.

ADRIANA
Why, so I did.

ABBESS
                              Ay, but not rough enough.

ABBESS

> Be quiet, people! Why have you come here in such a mob?

ADRIANA

> To get my poor, mad husband out from inside there. Let us in so we can tie him up tight and bring him home to recover.

ANGELO

> (to SECOND MERCHANT) I knew he wasn't quite in his right mind.

SECOND MERCHANT

> (to ANGELO) Now I'm sorry I raised my sword against him.

ABBESS

> How long has he been possessed like this?

ADRIANA

> This week he was sad, moody, and depressed and very different from his usual self. But it wasn't until this afternoon that he broke out into violence.

ABBESS

> Did he lose a lot of money in a shipwreck? Has a close friend of his died? Has he fallen in love with another woman? That's a sin young men often commit because they allow their eyes to wander. Which of these bad things happened to him?

ADRIANA

> None of them, except the last one. He fell in love, and that made him leave home often.

ABBESS

> You should have reprimanded him for that.

ADRIANA

> I did.

ABBESS

> Fine, but you weren't harsh enough.

ADRIANA
As roughly as my modesty would let me.

ABBESS
60   Haply in private.

ADRIANA
And in assemblies too.

ABBESS
Ay, but not enough.

ADRIANA
It was the copy of our conference.
In bed he slept not for my urging it;
At board he fed not for my urging it.
65   Alone, it was the subject of my theme;
In company I often glancèd it.
Still did I tell him it was vile and bad.

ABBESS
And thereof came it that the man was mad.
The venom clamors of a jealous woman
70   Poisons more deadly than a mad dog's tooth.
It seems his sleeps were hinder'd by thy railing,
And therefore comes it that his head is light.
Thou sayst his meat was sauced with thy upbraidings.
Unquiet meals make ill digestions.
75   Thereof the raging fire of fever bred,
And what's a fever but a fit of madness?
Thou sayest his sports were hinderd by thy brawls.
Sweet recreation barred, what doth ensue
But moody and dull melancholy,
80   Kinsman to grim and comfortless despair,
And at her heels a huge infectious troop
Of pale distemperatures and foes to life?
In food, in sport, and life-preserving rest
To be disturbed, would mad or man or beast.
85   The consequence is, then, thy jealous fits
Have scared thy husband from the use of wits.

ADRIANA

I was as harsh as I could be while still being a lady.

ABBESS

You scolded him in private?

ADRIANA

And in public too.

ABBESS

Fine, but not enough.

ADRIANA

It was all we talked about. I kept him awake at night talking about it. He couldn't eat without me talking about it. When we were alone, it was the only thing I talked about, and when we were with other people, I often found a way to mention it. All I ever did was tell him how hurtful and bad it was.

ABBESS

And that's why he went crazy. A jealous woman's poisonous ranting is worse than the bite of a rabid dog. You disturbed his sleep with your complaining, which is why he's disoriented. You seasoned his food with screams. Stress during mealtime ruins the digestion, and that gave him a raging fever. Fever, as we know, is a kind of madness. You spoiled his fun by fighting with him, and when people can't enjoy themselves, they grow moody and dull with melancholy—they come very close to being grim and cheerlessly depressed. Next thing you know, all kinds of terrible illnesses break out. Ruining his meals, his enjoyment, and his sleep would drive any man or beast mad. What I'm saying is, your jealousy has pushed your husband away from his sanity.

LUCIANA
> She never reprehended him but mildly
> When he demeaned himself rough, rude, and wildly.—
> *(to* ADRIANA*)* Why bear you these rebukes and answer not?

ADRIANA
90
> She did betray me to my own reproof.
> Good people, enter and lay hold on him.

ABBESS
> No, not a creature enters in my house.

ADRIANA
> Then let your servants bring my husband forth.

ABBESS
> Neither: he took this place for sanctuary,
95
> And it shall privilege him from your hands
> Till I have brought him to his wits again
> Or lose my labor in assaying it.

ADRIANA
> I will attend my husband, be his nurse,
> Diet his sickness, for it is my office
100
> And will have no attorney but myself;
> And therefore let me have him home with me.

ABBESS
> Be patient, for I will not let him stir
> Till I have used the approvd means I have,
> With wholesome syrups, drugs, and holy prayers,
105
> To make of him a formal man again.
> It is a branch and parcel of mine oath,
> A charitable duty of my order.
> Therefore depart and leave him here with me.

ADRIANA
> I will not hence and leave my husband here;
110
> And ill it doth beseem your holiness
> To separate the husband and the wife.

LUCIANA

She was always gentle when she scolded him, even when he behaved in the worst and wildest ways. *(to* **ADRIANA***)* Why won't you defend yourself against this woman?

ADRIANA

She has tricked me into seeing my own faults. Gentlemen, go in there and grab him.

ABBESS

Nobody goes into my house!

ADRIANA

Then have your servants bring him out.

ABBESS

In Shakespeare's period, people who sought protection in churches and other holy places were considered outside the reach of the law.

No: he came here for sanctuary, and that will protect him from you. I'll try to bring him back to his right mind and work to the end of my abilities to do so.

ADRIANA

It's my place to take care of my husband and nurse him back to health. It is my duty and mine alone. So let me take him home.

ABBESS

Be patient. I'm not going to let him leave until I've tried every means to cure him. With my healthful potions, drugs, and holy prayers, I'll make him a complete man again. Healing is part and parcel of my religious vows; it is a charitable duty my order performs. Therefore, depart, and leave him here with me.

ADRIANA

I will not depart and leave my husband here. It doesn't suit your holiness to separate a husband and his wife.

ABBESS
  Be quiet and depart. Thou shalt not have him.

             Exit ABBESS

LUCIANA
  Complain unto the Duke of this indignity.

ADRIANA
  Come, go. I will fall prostrate at his feet
115 And never rise until my tears and prayers
  Have won his grace to come in person hither
  And take perforce my husband from the Abbess.

SECOND MERCHANT
  By this, I think, the dial points at five.
  Anon, I'm sure, the Duke himself in person
120 Comes this way to the melancholy vale,
  The place of death and sorry execution
  Behind the ditches of the abbey here.

ANGELO
  Upon what cause?

SECOND MERCHANT
  To see a reverend Syracusian merchant,
125 Who put unluckily into this bay
  Against the laws and statutes of this town,
  Beheaded publicly for his offense.

ANGELO
  See where they come. We will behold his death.

LUCIANA
  Kneel to the Duke before he pass the abbey.

Enter the DUKE OF EPHESUS *and* EGEON *the merchant of*
Syracuse, bare head, with the headsman and other officers

DUKE
130 Yet once again proclaim it publicly,
  If any friend will pay the sum for him,
  He shall not die; so much we tender him.

ABBESS

> Be quiet and depart. You're not going to take him.
>
> *The* ABBESS *exits.*

LUCIANA

> Go lodge a complaint about this with the duke.

ADRIANA

> Come with me. I'll fall at his feet and lie there until my pleading and crying convinces the duke to come here and force my husband to leave this abbey.

SECOND MERCHANT

> It's almost five o'clock. The duke will pass by here soon. He always passes here on his way to that melancholy place where criminals are put to death. It's just behind this abbey.

ANGELO

> Why is he going there today?

SECOND MERCHANT

> To see an elderly, unlucky merchant from Syracuse publicly beheaded for breaking the law and coming here to Ephesus.

ANGELO

> Here they come. We will watch the execution.

LUCIANA

> Kneel down to the duke before he passes by the abbey.

> *The* DUKE *enters with* EGEON, *who is bareheaded. The executioner and other officers follow.*

DUKE

> One more time, we proclaim this publicly: If anyone will pay this man's bail, he will not be put to death. This is how well we regard him.

ADRIANA
Justice, most sacred duke, against the Abbess.

DUKE
She is a virtuous and a reverend lady.
135   It cannot be that she hath done thee wrong.

ADRIANA
May it please your Grace, Antipholus my husband,
Whom I made lord of me and all I had
At your important letters, this ill day
A most outrageous fit of madness took him,
140   That desp'rately he hurried through the street,
With him his bondman, all as mad as he,
Doing displeasure to the citizens
By rushing in their houses, bearing thence
Rings, jewels, any thing his rage did like.
145   Once did I get him bound and sent him home
Whilst to take order for the wrongs I went
That here and there his fury had committed.
Anon, I wot not by what strong escape,
He broke from those that had the guard of him,
150   And with his mad attendant and himself,
Each one with ireful passion, with drawn swords,
Met us again and, madly bent on us,
Chased us away, till, raising of more aid,
We came again to bind them. Then they fled
155   Into this abbey, whither we pursued them,
And here the Abbess shuts the gates on us
And will not suffer us to fetch him out,
Nor send him forth that we may bear him hence.
Therefore, most gracious duke, with thy command
160   Let him be brought forth and borne hence for help.

DUKE
Long since thy husband served me in my wars,
And I to thee engaged a prince's word,
When thou didst make him master of thy bed,
To do him all the grace and good I could.

ADRIANA

Duke, the abbess has wronged me and I seek justice.

DUKE

She's a virtuous and holy lady. She can't possibly have done you any wrong.

ADRIANA

Your Highness, you were the one who introduced me to my husband, Antipholus, and suggested I marry him. On this terrible day, a most outrageous fit of madness possessed him. It made him run desperately through the streets with his servant, who is just as mad. He angered all the citizens by rushing into their houses and taking rings, jewels, and anything else he felt like. At one point I managed to get him tied up and sent home so that I could make some order out of all the trouble he caused. But somehow, he broke free from his guards. Then he and his crazy servant found us and chased us away with swords. We got more help and came back to capture them, but then they fled into this abbey. We tried to go in, but the abbess stopped us. She wouldn't let us get him and she wouldn't send him out. So please, most gracious duke, order her to bring him out so we can get him some help.

DUKE

A long time ago your husband was a soldier in the wars I led. And when you married him and made him the master of your bed, I gave you my word that I would do everything I possibly could for him.

165   Go, some of you, knock at the abbey gate,
            And bid the Lady Abbess come to me.
            I will determine this before I stir.

Enter a MESSENGER

MESSENGER
            O mistress, mistress, shift and save yourself.
            My master and his man are both broke loose,
170   Beaten the maids a-row, and bound the doctor,
            Whose beard they have singed off with brands of fire,
            And ever as it blazed, they threw on him
            Great pails of puddled mire to quench the hair.
            My master preaches patience to him, and the while
175   His man with scissors nicks him like a fool;
            And sure, unless you send some present help,
            Between them they will kill the conjurer.

ADRIANA
            Peace, fool. Thy master and his man are here,
            And that is false thou dost report to us.

MESSENGER
180   Mistress, upon my life I tell you true.
            I have not breathed almost since I did see it.
            He cries for you, and vows, if he can take you,
            To scorch your face and to disfigure you.

Cry within

            Hark, hark, I hear him, mistress. Fly, begone!

DUKE
185   Come, stand by me. Fear nothing.—Guard with halberds.

Enter ANTIPHOLUS OF EPHESUS *and* DROMIO OF EPHESUS

(to his followers) Go, knock on the gate and bid the abbess come out here and speak to me. I'll settle this before I go.

A MESSENGER *enters.*

MESSENGER

Mistress! Run and save yourself. My master and his servant broke loose. They've beaten the maids and tied up Doctor Pinch. Then they set fire to his beard and threw sewage to put out the flames. My master keeps telling the doctor to relax, while his servant cuts the doctor's hair in a ridiculous fashion. If you don't send some help, they'll kill Doctor Pinch.

ADRIANA

Shut up, fool! Your master and his servant are here. You're telling a lie.

MESSENGER

Mistress, I swear on my life that it's true. It was just moments ago. He's crying out for you and swears he'll burn your face and disfigure you if he can get ahold of you.

Shouts are heard from offstage.

Listen, listen! I hear him, mistress. Run, get out of here!

DUKE

(to ADRIANA*)* Stand with me. Don't be scared. *(to his men)* Guards, get your weapons!

ANTIPHOLUS OF EPHESUS *and* DROMIO OF EPHESUS *enter.*

ADRIANA
> Ay me, it is my husband. Witness you
> That he is borne about invisible.
> Even now we housed him in the abbey here,
> And now he's there, past thought of human reason.

ANTIPHOLUS OF EPHESUS
190
> Justice, most gracious duke, O, grant me justice,
> Even for the service that long since I did thee
> When I bestrid thee in the wars and took
> Deep scars to save thy life. Even for the blood
> That then I lost for thee, now grant me justice.

EGEON
195
> *(aside)* Unless the fear of death doth make me dote,
> I see my son Antipholus and Dromio.

ANTIPHOLUS OF EPHESUS
> Justice, sweet prince, against that woman there,
> She whom thou gav'st to me to be my wife,
> That hath abusèd and dishonored me
200
> Even in the strength and height of injury.
> Beyond imagination is the wrong
> That she this day hath shameless thrown on me.

DUKE
> Discover how, and thou shalt find me just.

ANTIPHOLUS OF EPHESUS
> This day, great duke, she shut the doors upon me
205
> While she with harlots feasted in my house.

DUKE
> A grievous fault.—Say, woman, didst thou so?

ADRIANA
> No, my good lord. Myself, he, and my sister
> Today did dine together. So befall my soul
> As this is false he burdens me withal.

LUCIANA
210
> Ne'er may I look on day, nor sleep on night
> But she tells to your Highness simple truth.

ADRIANA

Oh, my, it's my husband. Look, he can become invisible. Just now we put him in the abbey over here, and now he's over there. It's impossible to understand.

ANTIPHOLUS OF EPHESUS

Justice, gracious duke. Please bring me justice! A long time ago I did good service to you. I fought in your wars and took deep wounds to save your life. In exchange for the blood I shed for you then, I ask you for justice now.

EGEON

(to himself) The fear of death might be making me senile, but I think I see my son Antipholus, and Dromio.

ANTIPHOLUS OF EPHESUS

Sweet prince, I want justice from that woman there. This woman that you urged me to marry has abused me and dishonored me, doing the most injury possible. The things she has shamelessly hurled on me are beyond imagination.

DUKE

Tell me the details. You know I'll be fair.

ANTIPHOLUS OF EPHESUS

Today, great duke, she locked me out of my house and feasted there with whores.

DUKE

That's terrible! *(to ADRIANA)* Tell us, woman, did you do that?

ADRIANA

No, my good lord. I ate with him and my sister. Damn my soul if these accusations are true!

LUCIANA

If she's lying, I pray that I never sleep again at night or wake up during the day.

ANGELO
> O perjured woman! —They are both forsworn.
> In this the madman justly chargeth them.

ANTIPHOLUS OF EPHESUS
> My liege, I am advisèd what I say,
> Neither disturbed with the effect of wine,
> Nor heady-rash, provoked with raging ire,
> Albeit my wrongs might make one wiser mad.
> This woman locked me out this day from dinner.
> That goldsmith there, were he not packed with her,
> Could witness it, for he was with me then,
> Who parted with me to go fetch a chain,
> Promising to bring it to the Porpentine,
> Where Balthasar and I did dine together.
> Our dinner done and he not coming thither,
> I went to seek him. In the street I met him,
> And in his company that gentleman. *(points to the* SECOND
>   MERCHANT*)*
> There did this perjured goldsmith swear me down
> That I this day of him received the chain,
> Which, God he knows, I saw not; for the which
> He did arrest me with an officer.
> I did obey, and sent my peasant home
> For certain ducats. He with none returned.
> Then fairly I bespoke the officer
> To go in person with me to my house.
> By th' way we met
> My wife, her sister, and a rabble more
> Of vile confederates. Along with them
> They brought one Pinch, a hungry, lean-faced villain,
> A mere anatomy, a mountebank,
> A threadbare juggler, and a fortune-teller,
> A needy, hollow-eyed, sharp-looking wretch,
> A living dead man. This pernicious slave,
> Forsooth, took on him as a conjurer,
> And, gazing in mine eyes, feeling my pulse,

NO FEAR SHAKESPEARE

ANGELO

Oh, lying woman! Both of them are liars: the madman accuses them justly.

ANTIPHOLUS OF EPHESUS

My lord, I know what I'm saying. I'm not drunk, and I haven't gone mad from anger—even though the wrongs done to me today would drive any man insane. This woman locked me out of the house today at lunchtime, and if he weren't conspiring with her, this jeweler could confirm my story since he was with me at the time. He left to fetch a necklace and he promised to bring it to the Porcupine, where I was dining with Balthasar. He hadn't arrived by the time we finished eating, so I went out looking for him. I met him in the street—he was there with that man. *(points to the* SECOND MERCHANT*)*

That's when this lying jeweler swore that he had already given me the necklace, which, God knows, he hadn't. He had me arrested for it, and I went with the officer, sending my servant home to get money for the bail. When my servant returned empty-handed, I politely asked the officer to accompany me to my house. On the way, we came across my wife, her sister, and their gang of vile associates.

One of them was a man named Pinch: a hungry, narrow-faced villain; a skeleton; a fraud; a raggedy magician and fortune-teller; a needy, hollow-eyed, emaciated wretch; a walking corpse. He pretended to be some kind of sorcerer, and he gazed in my eyes and took my pulse. Then, with his thin face leering down at mine, he cried out that I was possessed.

245 And with no face (as 'twere) outfacing me,
Cries out I was possessed. Then all together
They fell upon me, bound me, bore me thence,
And in a dark and dankish vault at home
There left me and my man, both bound together,
250 Till gnawing with my teeth my bonds in sunder,
I gained my freedom and immediately
Ran hither to your Grace, whom I beseech
To give me ample satisfaction
For these deep shames and great indignities.

ANGELO
255 My lord, in truth, thus far I witness with him:
That he dined not at home, but was locked out.

DUKE
But had he such a chain of thee or no?

ANGELO
He had, my lord, and when he ran in here,
These people saw the chain about his neck.

SECOND MERCHANT
260 Besides, I will be sworn these ears of mine
Heard you confess you had the chain of him
After you first forswore it on the mart,
And thereupon I drew my sword on you,
And then you fled into this abbey here,
265 From whence I think you are come by miracle.

ANTIPHOLUS OF EPHESUS
I never came within these abbey walls,
Nor ever didst thou draw thy sword on me.
I never saw the chain, so help me heaven,
And this is false you burden me withal.

DUKE
270 Why, what an intricate impeach is this!
I think you all have drunk of Circe's cup.
If here you housed him, here he would have been.
(to ADRIANA) If he were mad, he would not plead so coldly.

Then they all pounced on me, tied me up, carried me away, and left me in a dark, dank cellar in my house. They left me and my servant there, tied together. Eventually I chewed through the ropes and freed myself, and I immediately ran to find you, Your Grace. I beg you: grant me justice for the deep shame I have suffered and the terrible wrongs done to me.

ANGELO

Your Highness, I can confirm this much: he was locked out of his house and didn't eat at home.

DUKE

But did he receive a necklace from you?

ANGELO

He did, my lord. And when he ran in here, everyone could see that he was wearing that necklace.

SECOND MERCHANT

Besides, I'll swear I heard you confess that you *did* receive the necklace, even after you swore at the marketplace that you hadn't. That's when I raised my sword against you, and you fled into this abbey—which, I think, you must have escaped from through some kind of trick.

ANTIPHOLUS OF EPHESUS

I was never inside this abbey, and you never raised your sword against me. I never saw the necklace, so help me heaven! Everything you charge me with is untrue.

DUKE

Why, what a complicated case this is! I think you all must have drunk some kind of potion that's turned you all into animals. *(to* ADRIANA*)* If you put him in the abbey, that's where he'd be. If he were insane, he wouldn't be pleading his case so sensibly. You say he

You say he dined at home; the goldsmith here
275   Denies that saying. Sirrah, what say you?

DROMIO OF EPHESUS
Sir, he dined with her there, at the Porpentine.

COURTESAN
He did, and from my finger snatched that ring.

ANTIPHOLUS OF EPHESUS
'Tis true, my liege; this ring I had of her.

DUKE
Saw'st thou him enter at the abbey here?

COURTESAN
280   As sure, my liege, as I do see your Grace.

DUKE
Why, this is strange.—Go call the Abbess hither.
I think you are all mated or stark mad.

Exit one to ABBESS

EGEON
Most mighty duke, vouchsafe me speak a word.
Haply I see a friend will save my life
285   And pay the sum that may deliver me.

DUKE
Speak freely, Syracusian, what thou wilt.

EGEON
(to ANTIPHOLUS OF EPHESUS*)* Is not your name, sir, called
    Antipholus?
And is not that your bondman Dromio?

DROMIO OF EPHESUS
Within this hour I was his bondman sir,
290   But he, I thank him, gnawed in two my cords.
Now am I Dromio, and his man, unbound.

EGEON
I am sure you both of you remember me.

DROMIO OF EPHESUS
Ourselves we do remember, sir, by you.
For lately we were bound as you are now.
295   You are not Pinch's patient, are you, sir?

sirrah = term
of address for a
person of low
social standing

ate at home, but the jeweler says he didn't. Sirrah, what do you have to say?

DROMIO OF EPHESUS

Sir, he ate with this woman at the Porcupine.

COURTESAN

He did, and he snatched my ring right off my finger.

ANTIPHOLUS OF EPHESUS

That's true, my lord: I did get this ring from her.

DUKE

Did you see him enter this abbey?

COURTESAN

As clearly as I see you, my lord.

DUKE

This is very odd. Get the abbess out here. I think you're all either bewildered or stark raving mad.

Someone exits to get the **ABBESS**.

EGEON

Mighty duke, please allow me to say something. I think I see a friend who will pay my bail and save my life.

DUKE

Feel free to say what you wish, Syracusian.

EGEON

(*to* **ANTIPHOLUS OF EPHESUS**) Isn't your name Antipholus? And isn't that Dromio, the man bound to you?

DROMIO OF EPHESUS

I was bound to him an hour ago, sir, but thankfully he chewed through our ropes. Now I'm Dromio and no longer attached to him.

EGEON

I'm sure you both remember me.

DROMIO OF EPHESUS

Actually, it's ourselves you bring to mind since just a few moments ago we were tied up, as you are now. You're not one of Pinch's patients, are you, sir?

EGEON
Why look you strange on me? You know me well.

ANTIPHOLUS OF EPHESUS
I never saw you in my life till now.

EGEON
O, grief hath changed me since you saw me last,
And careful hours with time's deformèd hand
300   Have written strange defeatures in my face.
But tell me yet, dost thou not know my voice?

ANTIPHOLUS OF EPHESUS
Neither.

EGEON
Dromio, nor thou?

DROMIO OF EPHESUS
                    No, trust me, sir, nor I.

EGEON
I am sure thou dost.

DROMIO OF EPHESUS
305   Ay, sir, but I am sure I do not, and whatsoever a man denies,
you are now bound to believe him.

EGEON
Not know my voice! O time's extremity,
Hast thou so crack'd and splitted my poor tongue
In seven short years that here my only son
310   Knows not my feeble key of untuned cares?
Though now this grainèd face of mine be hid
In sap-consuming winter's drizzled snow,
And all the conduits of my blood froze up,
Yet hath my night of life some memory,
315   My wasting lamps some fading glimmer left,
My dull deaf ears a little use to hear.
All these old witnesses—I cannot err—
Tell me thou art my son Antipholus.

EGEON

> Why are you looking at me so strangely? You know me well.

ANTIPHOLUS OF EPHESUS

> I never saw you before in my life.

EGEON

> Oh, grief has transformed me since the last time you saw me. Time has the power to deform people, and the sorrowful hours I have spent in his company have put these strange lines and wrinkles on my face. But tell me this: don't you know my voice?

ANTIPHOLUS OF EPHESUS

> No.

EGEON

> Don't you, Dromio?

DROMIO OF EPHESUS

> No sir, trust me, I do not.

EGEON

> I am sure you do.

DROMIO OF EPHESUS

> Fine, sir, but I'm sure I don't. And you're in no position to doubt my word.

EGEON

> You don't know my voice? Oh, severe Time! Have you mangled my tongue so badly in these seven short years that my only son can no longer recognize my weak, sorrow-ravaged voice? It's true: this aged face of mine is hidden by a snow white beard, and the blood is freezing in my veins. But I still have a little memory left, and there's still some fire in my eyes; my dull, deaf ears can still hear a little. All these aging faculties tell me—and I cannot be wrong—that you are my son, Antipholus.

ANTIPHOLUS OF EPHESUS
> I never saw my father in my life.

EGEON
320
> But seven years since, in Syracusa, boy,
> Thou know'st we parted. But perhaps, my son,
> Thou sham'st to acknowledge me in misery.

ANTIPHOLUS OF EPHESUS
> The Duke and all that know me in the city
> Can witness with me that it is not so
325
> I ne'er saw Syracusa in my life.

DUKE
> I tell thee, Syracusian, twenty years
> Have I been patron to Antipholus,
> During which time he ne'er saw Syracusa.
> I see thy age and dangers make thee dote.

Enter the ABBESS *with* ANTIPHOLUS OF SYRACUSE
and DROMIO OF SYRACUSE

ABBESS
330
> Most mighty duke, behold a man much wronged.

All gather to see them

ADRIANA
> I see two husbands, or mine eyes deceive me.

DUKE
> *(looks at the* ANTIPHOLUS *twins)* One of these men is genius
>   to the other.
> *(looks at the* DROMIO *twins)* And so, of these, which is the
>   natural man
> And which the spirit? Who deciphers them?

DROMIO OF SYRACUSE
335
> I, sir, am Dromio. Command him away.

ANTIPHOLUS OF EPHESUS

> I never saw my father in my life.

EGEON

> You know that we parted only seven years ago, in Syracuse. Maybe you're ashamed to admit that you know me because I'm a prisoner now.

ANTIPHOLUS OF EPHESUS

> The duke and everyone who knows me in this city can confirm that's not true. I've never been to Syracuse in my life.

DUKE

> I tell you, Syracusian. I've been looking after Antipholus for twenty years, and during that time he's never been to Syracuse. Your old age and the prospect of death are making you imagine things.

> *The* ABBESS *enters, along with* ANTIPHOLUS OF SYRACUSE *and* DROMIO OF SYRACUSE.

ABBESS

> Mighty duke, look here and see a man who's been treated most terribly!

> *Everyone gathers around to look.*

ADRIANA

> Either my eyes deceive me, or I see two husbands.

DUKE

> *(looks at the* ANTIPHOLUS *twins)* One of these men is the other's genius. *(looks at the* DROMIO *twins)* And the same with these two. But which is the man and which is the spirit? Can anyone tell?

genius = attendant spirit, believed to follow a person throughout his life

DROMIO OF SYRACUSE

> I, sir, am Dromio. Command this man to leave.

DROMIO OF EPHESUS
I, sir, am Dromio. Pray, let me stay.

ANTIPHOLUS OF SYRACUSE
Egeon art thou not, or else his ghost?

DROMIO OF SYRACUSE
O, my old master.—Who hath bound him here?

ABBESS
Whoever bound him, I will loose his bonds
340 And gain a husband by his liberty.—
Speak, old Egeon, if thou be'st the man
That hadst a wife once called Emilia,
That bore thee at a burden two fair sons.
O, if thou be'st the same Egeon, speak,
345 And speak unto the same Emilia.

DUKE
Why, here begins his morning story right;
These two Antipholuses, these two so like,
And these two Dromios, one in semblance—
Besides her urging of her wreck at sea—
350 These are the parents to these children,
Which accidentally are met together.

EGEON
If I dream not, thou art Emilia.
If thou art she, tell me where is that son
That floated with thee on the fatal raft?

ABBESS
355 By men of Epidamnum he and I
And the twin Dromio all were taken up;
But by and by rude fishermen of Corinth
By force took Dromio and my son from them
And me they left with those of Epidamnum.
360 What then became of them I cannot tell;
I to this fortune that you see me in.

DUKE
(to ANTIPHOLUS OF SYRACUSE) Antipholus, thou cam'st
from Corinth first.

DROMIO OF EPHESUS

I, sir, am Dromio. Please, let me stay.

ANTIPHOLUS OF SYRACUSE

You are Egeon, aren't you? Or are you his ghost?

DROMIO OF SYRACUSE

Oh, my old master!—Who tied him up?

ABBESS

Whoever tied him up, I will loosen the ropes, and with his freedom I will gain a husband. Tell us, old Egeon: are you the man who once had a wife named Emilia, who gave birth to two fair sons? Oh, if you are the same Egeon, speak now, and speak to that same Emilia!

DUKE

Why, now the story the merchant told me this morning is starting to make sense. These two Antipholuses, who look so alike—and these two Dromios, who seem to have the same face—and her story of being shipwrecked—why, these two are the parents of these children and have been reunited by accident.

EGEON

If I'm not dreaming, you are Emilia. If it's really you, tell me what happened to our son, who floated away with you on that deadly raft.

ABBESS

Some men from Epidamnum rescued me, our son, and Dromio. But then a gang of violent fishermen from Corinth kidnapped Dromio and my son and carried them away. I don't know what became of them. You can see what became of me.

DUKE

Antipholus, aren't you originally from Corinth?

ANTIPHOLUS OF SYRACUSE
No, sir, not I. I came from Syracuse.

DUKE
Stay, stand apart. I know not which is which.

ANTIPHOLUS OF EPHESUS
365   I came from Corinth, my most gracious lord.

DROMIO OF EPHESUS
And I with him.

ANTIPHOLUS OF EPHESUS
Brought to this town by that most famous warrior
Duke Menaphon, your most renownèd uncle.

ADRIANA
Which of you two did dine with me today?

ANTIPHOLUS OF SYRACUSE
370   I, gentle mistress.

ADRIANA
                              And are not you my husband?

ANTIPHOLUS OF EPHESUS
No, I say nay to that.

ANTIPHOLUS OF SYRACUSE
And so do I, yet did she call me so,
And this fair gentlewoman, her sister here,
Did call me brother. *(to* LUCIANA*)* What I told you then
375   I hope I shall have leisure to make good,
If this be not a dream I see and hear.

ANGELO
That is the chain, sir, which you had of me.

ANTIPHOLUS OF SYRACUSE
I think it be, sir. I deny it not.

ANTIPHOLUS OF EPHESUS
And you, sir, for this chain arrested me.

ANGELO
380   I think I did, sir. I deny it not.

ANTIPHOLUS OF SYRACUSE

> No, sir. I came from Syracuse.

DUKE

> Wait, don't stand next to each other. I can't tell who's who.

ANTIPHOLUS OF EPHESUS

> I came from Corinth, Your Highness.

DROMIO OF EPHESUS

> And I came with him.

ANTIPHOLUS OF EPHESUS

> Your renowned uncle, Duke Menaphon, the famous soldier, brought me here.

ADRIANA

> Which of you two ate lunch with me today?

ANTIPHOLUS OF SYRACUSE

> I did, kind lady.

ADRIANA

> And you're my husband, right?

ANTIPHOLUS OF EPHESUS

> No, he's not. I say no to that.

ANTIPHOLUS OF SYRACUSE

> So do I, although she called me her husband. And this beautiful gentlewoman, her sister, called me brother. *(to* LUCIANA*)* If all this is for real, I hope I'll get the chance to make good on all the things I said to you today.

ANGELO

> That's the necklace I gave you, sir.

ANTIPHOLUS OF SYRACUSE

> I think it is, sir. I don't deny it.

ANTIPHOLUS OF EPHESUS

> And you, sir, had me arrested over that necklace.

ANGELO

> I think I did, sir. I don't deny it.

ADRIANA
I sent you money, sir, to be your bail
By Dromio, but I think he brought it not.

DROMIO OF EPHESUS
No, none by me.

ANTIPHOLUS OF SYRACUSE
This purse of ducats I received from you,
385   And Dromio my man did bring them me.
I see we still did meet each other's man,
And I was ta'en for him, and he for me,
And thereupon these errors are arose.

ANTIPHOLUS OF EPHESUS
These ducats pawn I for my father here.

DUKE
390   It shall not need. Thy father hath his life.

COURTESAN
Sir, I must have that diamond from you.

ANTIPHOLUS OF EPHESUS
There, take it; and much thanks for my good cheer.

ABBESS
Renownèd duke, vouchsafe to take the pains
To go with us into the abbey here
395   And hear at large discoursed all our fortunes,
And all that are assembled in this place
That by this sympathizèd one day's error
Have suffered wrong. Go, keep us company,
And we shall make full satisfaction.—
400   Thirty-three years have I but gone in travail
Of you, my sons, and till this present hour
My heavy burden ne'er deliverèd.—
The Duke, my husband, and my children both,
And you, the calendars of their nativity,
405   Go to a gossips' feast, and go with me.
After so long grief, such nativity!

DUKE
With all my heart I'll gossip at this feast.

ADRIANA

I sent Dromio to you with money for bail, but I don't think he brought it to you.

DROMIO OF EPHESUS

No, he didn't get any by me.

ANTIPHOLUS OF SYRACUSE

I got this purse full of money from you, and my Dromio brought it to me. It seems that we kept running into each other's servants all day. And everyone thought I was him, and he was me, and that's how all these errors came about.

ANTIPHOLUS OF EPHESUS

I want to use this money to set my father free.

DUKE

That's not necessary. I'm going to let him live.

COURTESAN

Sir, I must get that diamond ring back from you.

ANTIPHOLUS OF EPHESUS

There, take it, and thanks for taking such good care of me.

ABBESS

Renowned duke, please join us in the abbey, where we will discuss at length all that has happened to us. Everyone assembled here who has been troubled by the day's events join us as well, and we will straighten everything out. My sons, waiting to hear news of you has been like a second childbirth: this time, my labor lasted thirty-three years, and I am only now delivered of my heavy burden. Duke Solinus, my husband, and both my children—and you two Dromios, who marked the day of my sons' births with your own— come into the abbey with me for a new christening. After such a long period of grief, we will have such a celebration!

DUKE

With all my heart, I'll join you.

Exeunt; the two DROMIOS *and the two* ANTIPHOLUS
brothers remain behind.

DROMIO OF SYRACUSE
(*to* ANTIPHOLUS OF EPHESUS) Master, shall I fetch your stuff
from shipboard?

ANTIPHOLUS OF EPHESUS
Dromio, what stuff of mine hast thou embarked?

DROMIO OF SYRACUSE
410   Your goods that lay at host, sir, in the Centaur.

ANTIPHOLUS OF SYRACUSE
He speaks to me.—I am your master, Dromio.
Come, go with us. We'll look to that anon.
Embrace thy brother there. Rejoice with him.

Exeunt ANTIPHOLUS OF SYRACUSE *and*
ANTIPHOLUS OF EPHESUS

DROMIO OF SYRACUSE
415   There is a fat friend at your master's house
That kitchened me for you today at dinner.
She now shall be my sister, not my wife.

DROMIO OF EPHESUS
Methinks you are my glass, and not my brother:
I see by you I am a sweet-faced youth.
Will you walk in to see their gossiping?

420 **DROMIO OF SYRACUSE**
Not I, sir. You are my elder.

DROMIO OF EPHESUS
That's a question. How shall we try it?

DROMIO OF SYRACUSE
We'll draw cuts for the signior. Till then, lead thou first.

DROMIO OF EPHESUS
Nay, then, thus:
We came into the world like brother and brother,
And now let's go hand in hand, not one before another.

Exeunt

Everyone exits, except for the DROMIO *twins and the* ANTIPHOLUS *twins.*

DROMIO OF SYRACUSE

(to ANTIPHOLUS OF EPHESUS*)* Master, should I go get your luggage off the ship?

ANTIPHOLUS OF EPHESUS

Dromio, what stuff of mine did you put on a ship?

DROMIO OF SYRACUSE

The stuff you had at the Centaur, sir.

ANTIPHOLUS OF SYRACUSE

He means me. I'm your master, Dromio. Come inside with us: we'll deal with that later. Embrace your brother there, and rejoice with him.

ANTIPHOLUS OF SYRACUSE and ANTIPHOLUS
OF EPHESUS *exit.*

DROMIO OF SYRACUSE

You have a fat friend at your master's house: she took care of me in the kitchen today, thinking I was you. I guess now she's going to be my sister-in-law and not my wife.

DROMIO OF EPHESUS

I think you're my mirror, not my brother. And I can see by looking at you that I'm a pretty good-looking fellow. Do you want to go in and join the party?

DROMIO OF SYRACUSE

After you, sir. You're older than me.

DROMIO OF EPHESUS

That's a good point. How can we tell which of us is the oldest?

DROMIO OF SYRACUSE

We'll draw straws. Meanwhile, after you.

DROMIO OF EPHESUS

No, I'll tell you what. We came into the world as brother and brother, so now let's enter hand in hand—not one before the other.

They exit.

SPARKNOTES LITERATURE GUIDES

1984

The Adventures of
  Huckleberry Finn

The Adventures of Tom
  Sawyer

The Aeneid

All Quiet on the Western
  Front

And Then There Were
  None

Angela's Ashes

Animal Farm

Anna Karenina

Anne of Green Gables

Anthem

Antony and Cleopatra

Aristotle's Ethics

As I Lay Dying

As You Like It

Atlas Shrugged

The Autobiography of
  Malcolm X

The Awakening

The Bean Trees

The Bell Jar

Beloved

Beowulf

Billy Budd

Black Boy

Bless Me, Ultima

The Bluest Eye

Brave New World

The Brothers Karamazov

The Call of the Wild

Candide

The Canterbury Tales

Catch-22

The Catcher in the Rye

The Chocolate War

The Chosen

Cold Mountain

Cold Sassy Tree

The Color Purple

The Count of Monte
  Cristo

Crime and Punishment

The Crucible

Cry, the Beloved Country

Cyrano de Bergerac

David Copperfield

Death of a Salesman

The Death of Socrates

The Diary of a Young Girl

A Doll's House

Don Quixote

Dr. Faustus

Dr. Jekyll and Mr. Hyde

Dracula

Dune

Edith Hamilton's
  Mythology

Emma

Ethan Frome

Fahrenheit 451

Fallen Angels

A Farewell to Arms

Farewell to Manzanar

Flowers for Algernon

For Whom the Bell Tolls

The Fountainhead

Frankenstein

The Giver

The Glass Menagerie

Gone With the Wind

The Good Earth

The Grapes of Wrath

Great Expectations

The Great Gatsby

Grendel

Gulliver's Travels

Hamlet

The Handmaid's Tale

Hard Times

Harry Potter and the
  Sorcerer's Stone

Heart of Darkness

Henry IV, Part I

Henry V

Hiroshima

The Hobbit

The House of Seven
  Gables

I Know Why the Caged
  Bird Sings

The Iliad

Inferno

Inherit the Wind

Invisible Man

Jane Eyre

Johnny Tremain

The Joy Luck Club

Julius Caesar

The Jungle

The Killer Angels

King Lear

The Last of the Mohicans

Les Miserables

A Lesson Before Dying

The Little Prince

Little Women

Lord of the Flies

The Lord of the Rings

Macbeth

Madame Bovary

A Man for All Seasons

The Mayor of
  Casterbridge

The Merchant of Venice

A Midsummer Night's
  Dream

Moby Dick

Much Ado About Nothing

My Antonia

Narrative of the Life of
  Frederick Douglass

Native Son

The New Testament

Night

Notes from Underground

The Odyssey

The Oedipus Plays

Of Mice and Men

The Old Man and the Sea

The Old Testament

Oliver Twist

The Once and Future
  King

One Day in the Life of
  Ivan Denisovich

One Flew Over the
  Cuckoo's Nest

One Hundred Years of
  Solitude

Othello

Our Town

The Outsiders

Paradise Lost

A Passage to India

The Pearl

The Picture of Dorian
  Gray

Poe's Short Stories

A Portrait of the Artist as
  a Young Man

Pride and Prejudice

The Prince

A Raisin in the Sun

The Red Badge of
  Courage

The Republic

Richard III

Robinson Crusoe

Romeo and Juliet

The Scarlet Letter

A Separate Peace

Silas Marner

Sir Gawain and the Green
  Knight

Slaughterhouse-Five

Snow Falling on Cedars

Song of Solomon

The Sound and the Fury

Steppenwolf

The Stranger

Streetcar Named Desire

The Sun Also Rises

A Tale of Two Cities

The Taming of the Shrew

The Tempest

Tess of the d'Ubervilles

The Things They Carried

Their Eyes Were
  Watching God

Things Fall Apart

To Kill a Mockingbird

To the Lighthouse

Treasure Island

Twelfth Night

Ulysses

Uncle Tom's Cabin

Walden

War and Peace

Wuthering Heights

A Yellow Raft in Blue
  Water